The male psychic subject constitution in the Freudian theory

Henrique Guilherme Scatolin

1st Edition

GlobalSouth
P R E S S

For more information, please
contact info@globalsouthpress.com or go to
http://www.globalsouthpress.com/

The male psychic subject constitution
in the Freudian theory
By SCATOLIN, Henrique—1st ed. — 2016
Includes bibliographical references and index.
ISBN: 978-1-943350-41-4

1. Psychology — Freudian theory
2. Psychology— Movements

GlobalSouth
P R E S S

Bulent Acma, Ph.D.
Department of Economics, Anadolu University, Eskişehir, Turkey.
Flavio Saraiva, Ph.D.
Universidade Nacional de Brasília, Brasilia, Brazil.
Helmunt Schlenter, Ph.D.
Institute for Global Dialogue, Pretoria, South Africa.
Tullo Vigevani, Ph.D.
Sao Paulo State University, Sao Paulo, Brazil.
Monica Arruda Almeida, Ph. D.
Georgetown University, Washington, D.C., United States of America.
Yong J. Wang, Ph.D.
Ohio University, Columbus, United States of America.
Chih-yu Shih, Ph.D.
National Taiwan University (ROC), Taipei, Taiwan.
Irene Klumbies, Ph.D.
Jacobs University Bremen, Bremen, Germany.
Sai Felicia Krishna-Hensel, Ph.D.
Center Business and Econ. Develop., Auburn University at Montgomery, Montgomery, United States of America.
José Ãlvaro Moisés, Ph.D.
Universidade de São Paulo (USP), São Paulo, Brazil

Table of Contents

Presentation

Currently many young people have already heard about Freudian contributions to human sciences, and such contributions have put in check the Cartesian logic of western science, demonstrating a new vision of the human being. Such visions broke, therefore, with the puerile narcissist Cartesian logic in which we could dwell in a house that we already knew its own structure, or its simple pillars. At the end of the 19th century and early 20th century, with his contributions to the logic of desire and the drive, Freud brings us a new vision of man, causing a rupture in the mechanistic logic present at this time, providing the search for new knowledge. From the publishing of the book *The Interpretation of Dreams*, the neurotic symptoms gained new understandings and the desire range gains a new outline, breaking the psychiatric symptomatic discourse that persisted at this time.

Beginning with this context, and with reference to the current context of our civilization (after nearly 116 years of the first psychoanalytic pillars), this book focuses on Freud's contributions to the understanding of the male psychic subject in Freudian theory and is intended for young readers, beginners in the great ocean of this rich science named *Psychoanalysis*. This book, introductory to psychoanalytic concepts, aims to answer some very frequent questions among young people, new readers, who are in the education process, such as, for example, how

Freud understands the male subject constitution? How do drive and desires appear? What would be the castration complex and its intrinsic relationship with the Oedipus complex in the male subject? From these issues, I invite you to make a historical digression, returning to Freud's main works for answering to the questions above.

I point out that even a century after his discoveries Psychoanalysis has never been so present in the everyday scene, shining its knowledge to the new understanding of the social, educational and organizational phenomena. However, its primary source still is the clinic and this will be the starting point of this introductory book, returning to Freudian classic metapsychological texts, interlinking them with the understanding of contemporary psychoanalysts of Latin America. Good reading to all...

The male psychic subject constitution in the Freudian theory

As already pointed out in our introduction, this book will review Freudian metapsychology, focusing on the key concepts that allow the understanding of male psychic constitution in the works of Sigmund Freud.

In the early constitution of psychoanalytic theory, Freud begins to develop the first psychoanalytic concepts that support the understanding of the psychic subject constitution. In 1895, in the twenty-fourth letter to Fliess, he states:

> I am tormented by two objectives: examine the form that the mental functioning theory will assume […], and, secondly, extract from psychopathology an outcome to normal psychology. Actually, it is impossible to have a satisfactory general conception of neuropsychotic disorders if you cannot link it to clear assumptions about the normal mental processes […][1].

At this time, Freud is in the early days of the neurotic and normal processes studies and all his constructions are under the traumatic theory approach of neuroses, in which he declares that neuroses are caused by sexual trauma resulting from a real seduction (a type of sexual abuse) performed by a perverse adult against a child.

---

1   MASSON, Jefrey M. *The Complete Correspondence of Sigmund Freud to W. Fliess*. Rio de Janeiro: Imago, 1986, p.130.

In 1895, in the letter number 28 addressed to Fliess, Freud says: "[...] I started a brief summary to submit to your appraisal [...]"[2]. This summary would be the first outline of the *Project for a Scientific Psychology*, which would only be published in 1950, eleven years after his death.

It is in this text that Freud recognizes the importance of the presence of another (the mother or someone that may replace her) for the baby psychic development. So, he says:

> The neurons filling [...] it will result in an inclination to discharge, an urgency that is released via motor capacity [...]. But, no discharge can produce a relieving result. In this case, the stimulus is only likely to be abolished by means of an intervention. The human body is, at first, unable to promote this specific action. This is performed by someone else's help, when an experienced person is facing a child state for a discharge through the internal change [...]. This discharge via acquires, therefore, the very important secondary function of communication, and the initial helplessness of human beings is the primary source of all moral reasons [...]. The entire event then constitutes the experience of satisfaction [...][3].

At the beginning of the psychic constitution, the tension state present in the newborn – caused by the search for satisfaction of his libidinal and organic needs, such as hunger – tries to be released by means of a motor discharge, such as the screaming and crying, but no motor discharge is able, by itself, to relief the internal tension of the newborn. The baby is unable to promote any specific action that relieves this tension, thus requiring

2 Idem, p.140.
3 FREUD, Sigmund (1895). Project for a Scientific Psychology. *ESB*, vol. I, 1996, p.370.

the help of another person, i.e. the external aid of the mother or someone that may replace her. In this way, the satisfaction experience puts an end to the child internal tension through the mother (or substitute) external aid to her son, causing the more radical consequences in the development of an individual functions.

In 1900, in his book *The Interpretation of Dreams*, Freud resumes the concept of satisfaction experience, highlighting the establishment of the desire by means of this experience, as he says:

> [...] As a result of the link thus established, the next time that this need is awakened, there will be an immediate psychic motion that will seek to recatechize the mnemonic image of perception and re-evoke the perception itself, that is, restore the original satisfaction situation. A motion of this kind is what we call desire [...][4].

The experience of satisfaction allows the baby a perception of relief from his tension, which mnemonic image is linked to the mnemonic trace of the excitement caused by this need. When this need appears again, there is a psychic motion which will seek to hallucinatorilly reinvest the mnemonic image of the original perception, seeking to restore the original satisfaction situation. This psychic motion of Freud is called desire. Only this is capable of putting the psychic apparatus in motion, in accordance with the pleasure principle.

In 1911, Freud resumes this inaugural moment of psychism, adding the principle of reality to the principle of pleasure, as he says:

---

4 FREUD, Sigmund (1900). The Interpretation of Dreams. *ESB*, vol. V, 1996, p.594-595.

[...] It was just the absence of the expected satisfaction [...] that led to the abandonment of this attempt of satisfaction through hallucination [...]. A new principle of mental functioning was thus introduced; what was presented in mind was no longer the pleasant, but the real, even if it was unpleasant. This establishment of the principle of reality has proven to be a momentous step [...]. [5]

Shortly after birth, due to his internal needs, the baby seeks to hallucinatorilly reinvest in the pleasure experience previously experienced. Due to the disappointment, he abandons this attempt of pleasurable satisfaction through hallucination, entering on the scene the principle of reality. Therefore, the new demands of the outside world cause a succession of adaptations necessary to the psychic apparatus constitution, and the entrance of the principle of reality is essential for the child survival.

Regarding the satisfaction experience, the Brazilian psychoanalyst Violante interprets: "in my view, according to Freud, this is the inaugural moment of psyche and sexuality genesis, since, with the milk, the baby must ingest the maternal libido. Through the subsequent experiences of pleasure and displeasure in the relationship with the mother (or substitute) and, then with the father, the psychosexual constitution of the subject is continued"[6].

In another reading on this experience, the Uruguayan psychoanalyst Vinár understands that:

"the place that helplessness occupies in the development of Freudian thought [...] underlines its inaugural and founder character [...]. The helplessness is the initial term that raises in Freud a series of conceptual constructs

---

5 FREUD, Sigmund (1911). Formulations on the Two Principles of Mental Functioning. *ESB*, vol. XII, 1996, p.238.

6 VIOLANTE, M. Lucia Vieira. *Freudian Essays Around the Psychosexuality*. São Paulo: Via Lettera, 2004, p.36.

strictly rigorous among themselves (primary and second-ary processes, principles of pleasure and reality, identity of perception and thought [...]. Helplessness, defenseless-ness and extreme dependency, assignment of value to the first another that solves the 'need' or internal tension and the anguish that is intrinsic to it. With these items Freud built the model of the satisfaction experience [...]"[7].

The awakening of drives

During the psychic constitution, immediately after the first satisfaction experience, which establishes the desire in the baby, Freud highlights the importance of maternal care towards the newborn, pointing out the awakening of infantile sexuality through these first cares. When publishing the *Three Essays*, the master says:

> "the child dealing with the person who assists him is, for him, a constant source of excitement and sexual satisfaction from erogenous zones, and even more if this person – usually, the mother – admires the child with the feelings derived from her own sexual life: she touches, kisses and cradles him, and it is perfectly clear that she treats him as the replacement of a fully legitimate sexual object [...][8].

This means that, since the experience of satisfaction, many of the subsequent experiences of the baby (such as play-ing, feeding and resting) are not lonely, always needing the help of his mother or someone who may replace her. When caressing,

7 VIÑAR, Marcelo N. *Psychoanalysis Today: Problems of Clinical Theory Articulation*. Montevideo: Trilce, 2002, p.46-48, free translation.
8 FREUD, Sigmund (1905). Three Essays on the Theory of Sexuality. *ESB,* vol. VII, 1996, p. 210-211.

kissing, talking with her baby, the mother (or who may replace her) is so awakening his sexual drive or libido. These cares related to the baby body become endless source of pleasure, of sexual excitement and satisfaction of his erogenous zones. Therefore, during these first cares, it is vital that the baby may swallow, along with the milk, the maternal libido.

With the publishing of these *Three Essays*, in 1905 (and during its successive editions, over a period of twenty years, it is subjected to considerable changes and additions to the extent of the general evolution of the psychoanalytical theory), Freud draws a study on sexual drive[9] differently from the concept of biologists. With the description of sexual aberrations, and also through his detailed study about infantile sexuality, he criticizes the popular concept about sexuality that restricts it to the genitality and to the reproduction goal. Since the *Three Essays*, Freud postulates that sexuality is not restricted to genitality, and its purpose is the pleasure and not just procreation. So, unlike biology, Freud considers that all drive object is variable.

For Freud, "in psychoanalysis, the concept of what is sexual covers a lot more; he goes lower and also above its popular sense [...]. For this reason, we prefer to talk about psychosexuality emphasizing the point that the mental factor in the sex life should not be disdained or underestimated" [10]. Freud, throughout his work, maintains that the subject psychosexual constitution occurs

9 I would like to open a brief parenthesis and point out that James Strachey, along the Standard English Edition, translated by Trieb as Instinct, influencing the translation, in Portuguese language, of Instinct by Instinct. Unlike the English and Brazilian version, I reiterate that the understanding this book about drive is based on the French translation, when "the term *pulsion* was introduced in the French translations of Freud as the equivalent of the German Trieb". [LAPLANCHE, J. & PONTALIS, J-B. (1967). *Vocabulary of Psychoanalysis*. São Paulo: Martins Fontes, 2001, p. 394].

10 FREUD, Sigmund (1910). Sylvan Psychoanalysis. *ESB*, vol. XI, 1996, p. 234.

since extra uterine life. Psychoanalysis postulates the inseparability between psychism and sexuality, i.e., sexuality is conceived as constitutive of the psychic subject. Therefore, psychosexuality means that human sexuality has a psychic factor, in addition to the somatic, and libido or sexual drive and the drive of self-conservation constitute the life drive, which, beside the death drive, are an integral part of the psychism and of its operation.

In 1920, when publishing *Beyond the Principle of Pleasure*, Freud resumes the issue of drives, highlighting: "we [...] were taken to distinguish two species of instincts: those that seek to lead the living to death, and the others, the sexual instincts, which are perpetuating, trying and achieving a renewal of life [...]"[11]. With this work publishing, Freud established a new impulsive dualism, opposing the life drives to the death drives. From the observation about the compulsion to repetition (a compulsion that leads the subject to repeat painful situations, being this a replica of old experiences), Freud theorized about the death drive.

For Freud, the "emergence of life would be [...] the cause of life continuation and also, at the same time, the effort towards death. And life itself would be a conflict and a reconciliation of these two inclinations"[12]. As mentioned before, these two inclinations are two drive classes that coexist since birth: the life drive – Eros, sexual drive or libido and self-conservation drive – and the death drive – Thanatos, destructive drive, of domain or power desire.

Freud says that "both classes of instincts, both Eros and the instinct of death [...] would have been operating and working against each other since the first origin of life"[13]. The death drive – which is expressed by aggressive or destructive drives –

11 FREUD, Sigmund (1920). Op. cit. *ESB*, vol. XVIII, 1996, p. 57.
12 FREUD, Sigmund (1923). The Ego and the Id. *ESB*, vol. XIX, 1996, p.53.
13 FREUD, Sigmund (1923 [1922]). Two Encyclopedia Articles. *ESB*, vol. XVIII, p. 274.

and the life drive are, in general, amalgamated along the subject psychic constitution.

According to Freud, "in organisms [...], libido faces the instinct of death or destruction dominant in them [...]. Libido's mission is to make innocuous the destructor instinct and performs it diverting this instinct, in a large extent, outside [...] with the assistance of a special organic system, the muscular apparatus"[14]. The deviation of the death drive (destructive) is essential for the establishment of the psyche. The life drive aims to make the destructive and aggressive drive harmless, greatly directing it to outside and, partially, by mixing with it. If a part of this destructive drive is put at the service of sexual function, this part becomes the sadism itself; but if a part of this drive remains within the organism, this drive is libidinally trapped, giving rise to masochism. Among its manifestations, we can find the erogenous masochism (common in cases of perversion, where sexual pleasure is linked to pain), the female masochism (accessible by fantasies of masochistic men), and the moral masochism (and this latter is essential for understanding the unconscious feeling of guilt and the negative therapeutic reaction). So, the life and death drives are always mixed along the psychic constitution, and a fusion or de-fusion of these drives may occur.

Regarding the concept of life and death drives, Leplanche and Pontalis understand that:

> In the libidinal development of the individual, Freud described the combined game of life drive and death drive, both in its sadist form [...], and in its masochist form [...]. In fact, what Freud seeks to explicitly highlight with the expression 'death drive' is what is most fundamental in the concept of drive, the return to a previous state and, ultimately, the absolute return of the

14 FREUD, Sigmund (1924). The Economic Problem of Masochism. *ESB*, vol. XIX, 1996, p.181.

inorganic [...]. The latest formulations of Freud [...] indicate that the underlying principle to life drives is a binding principle [...]. The goal of the other drive [the death drive] is, on the other hand, dissolving the aggregates, and so destroying the things [...][15].

The relevance of the parents' presence at the beginning of psychic constitution

In addition to the life and death drives, which coexist since birth, Freud postulates that, at this beginning of live, "the child lips behave as an erogenous zone and the stimulation by the warm milk flow was no doubt the source of pleasurable sensation [...]. Sexual activity primarily relies on one of the functions that serve for the life preservation, and only later becomes independent from them [...]"[16]. Early in life, the baby sexual pleasure comes from the excitement of mouth, lips, tongue and etc. At this time, the sexual activity is related to the intake of milk and the lips stimulation. In addition to providing that sexual pleasure, the affectionate relationship between baby and mother becomes a prototype for all loving relationships in the adult life of this subject.

In 1914, in the paper *On Narcissism: An Introduction*, Freud reiterates the importance of maternal care in the first months of the baby life, noting that "the first sexual objects of a child are the people who care about his food, care and protection"[17]. These people can be the mother or who may replace her. This relationship established since the first moments of life

---

15 LAPLANCHE, J. & PONTALIS, J-B. (1967). *Vocabulary of Psychoanalysis*. São Paulo: Martins Fontes, 2001, p.408-415.

16 FREUD, Sigmund (1905). Three Essays on the Theory of Sexuality. *ESB,* vol. VII, 1996, p. 171.

17 FREUD, Sigmund (1914). Op. cit. *ESB*, vol. XV, 1996, p. 94.

becomes an object choice model established for adult life. This kind of object choice Freud calls anaclitic (or binding).

In addition to the anaclitic object choice, there is also the narcissistic object choice. Regarding this choice, Freud states that the person may love "what she herself is, [...] was, [...] would like to be or someone who was once part of herself"[18]. This means that the individual chooses according to the model of what his ego is, was, or would like to be, or also, according to the model of someone who once was part of his own ego, such as the phallic mother.

In his work *An Outline of Psychoanalysis*, Freud does not change his statements on the importance of maternal presence in the first moments of the psychic constitution, reiterating that "the first erotic object of a child is the mother's breast that feeds him; the origin of love is linked to the satisfied need of nutrition"[19]. Early in life, due to the care with the child body, the mother becomes his first seducer, i.e., his first erotic object, because in addition to meeting his physiological needs, these early care have awakened many pleasant and unpleasant physical sensations. So, in this dual relationship (mother-baby), the mother is the first object of desire, of love both for the boy and the girl.

The Argentinian psychoanalyst Silvia Bleichmar, in her interpretation about the importance of the role played by the mother in the boy psychic constitution, highlights that: "we know, since Freud, that initially the mother is, for both genders, the first love object, and we can say, with him, that the boy retains this object in the Oedipus complex [...]" [20].

Freud not only points out the importance of mother and of her care during the first moments of life, but also recognizes

18 FREUD, Sigmund (1914). On Narcissism: An Introduction. *ESB*, vol. XIV, 1996, p.84.

19 FREUD, Sigmund (1940[1938]). Op. cit. *ESB*, vol. XXIII, 1996, p.202.

20 BLEICHMAR, Silvia. *In the Origins of the Psychic Subject: from Myth to History*. Porto Alegre: Artes Médicas, p.187.

the importance of the paternal presence. In 1914, in the text *On Narcissism: An Introduction*, when addressing the affectionate father attitude towards his children, he highlights: "we must recognize that it is a revival and reproduction of his own narcissism and which he has long abandoned"[21]. The father is also present since the early psychic constitution of both the boy and the girl. When considering that the baby "will be once again the center and the core of creation – Your Majesty the Baby"[22], Freud postulates that the birth of a child represents for the couple (read here, father and mother) a revival of their own childish narcissism. During the care and attention that are intended for the baby, these parents assign all the perfections of the world to this new son, denying his defects and his imperfections.

The constitution of the ideal ego

Freud, in his text *On Narcissism: An Introduction*, in addition to pointing out the importance of the parents' presence in the child psychic constitution, also brings contributions to the ego constitution. For Freud, "a unit comparable to ego cannot exist in the individual since the beginning; ego has to be developed"[23]. At this point, Freud understands that the self-eroticism (that is, the manner how the sexual drives seeks satisfaction in the subject own body) is present since the beginning of psychic constitution, and the narcissism is a result of a new psychic action.

Before addressing this 'new psychic action', I would like to open a parenthesis and develop a brief digression on self-eroticism. In the letter 125 to Fliess, Freud already defined the self-eroticism as "a lower sexual layer […] that acts without any

---

21 FREUD, Sigmund (1914). Op. cit. *ESB*, vol. XV, 1996, p. 97.

22 Idem, p. 98.

23 Idem, p. 84.

psychosexual objective and only requires the local sensations of satisfaction"[24]. Six years after writing this letter, when writing the *Three Essays*, he postulates that, early in life, "the drive is not directed to another person; it is satisfied in the own body, it is self-erotic"[25]. So, the newborn shows a mode by which the sexual drive, connected to an organ or the excitement of an erogenous zone, finds satisfaction in a particular location of his own body. And this mode is referred to as self-eroticism. I close the parenthesis and return to the text *"On Narcissism: An Introduction"*.

It is necessary to highlight that, this text of 1914, although Freud did not define what would be this 'new psychic action', then, in the text *The Instinct and its Vicissitudes*, he explains that "at the very beginning of mental life, the ego is cathexized with instincts, and, to some extent, able to satisfy it in itself. We call this as 'narcissism' condition, and this form of obtaining satisfaction, as 'self-erotic'."[26] So, Freud highlights the narcissism as the initial phase of the ego development, a moment when the child loves herself. And due to the libidinal investment of parents, thanks to the overvaluation that governs the parents' attitude towards their children, bringing the children to the position of "your majesty, the baby", the ego in its earliest form as an ideal ego. Therefore, the ideal ego is the infantile ego that became target of self-love.

For Freud, before the ideal ego resulting in narcissism, the ego is "first and foremost, a bodily ego; and not simply a surface entity, but it is [...] the projection of a surface"[27]. Freud does not specify the date on which the ego is formed, but in a footnote

---

24 FREUD, Sigmund (1899). Letter of December 9. *ESB*, vol. I, 1996, p.331.

25 FREUD, Sigmund (1905). Three Essays on the Theory of Sexuality. *ESB*, vol. VII, 1996, p.170.

26 FREUD, Sigmund (1915). Op. cit. *ESB*, vol. XIV, 1996, p. 139.

27 FREUD, Sigmund (1923). The Ego and the Id. *ESB*, vol. XIX, 1996, p.40.

added to the English translation of 1927, he considers that the ego is derived from the bodily sensations from the body surface.

In his understanding about the ideal ego formation, the psychoanalyst Violante associates it with the entrance of the father figure, saying:

> [...] In his work, the father occupies a central place, although he [Freud] recognizes, later, the 'supreme importance' of the first relationships, almost exclusive, of the baby with the mother. So, this is how the father is present, since the first manner in which the ego is formed, as an ideal ego, being narcissistically invested, due to having been invested by the parents, when reliving the narcissism in the face of 'Your Majesty the Baby', as claimed by Freud in "On Narcissism'[...] Therefore, according to Freud, the entrance of the father in the familiar psychic environment occurs very early – if not from the beginning of the psychosexuality formation, since the early days of this formation.[28].

Pre-genital organizations

For Freud, if in the early psychic constitution, the baby has an id, and then, a bodily ego (derived from the bodily sensations), targeting to the formation of a narcissistically invested ideal ego, in the libidinal development level, the master states that, during the first years of a child life, there are "organizations of the sexual life in which genital areas have not assumed their predominant role yet"[29]. These organizations are defined

28 VIOLANTE, Maria Lucia Vieira. The Heirs of the Oedipus Complex. In: *Freudian Essays Around the Psychosexuality*. São Paulo: Via Leterra, 2004, p. 133.

29 FREUD, Sigmund (1905). Three Essays on the Theory of Sexua-

as pre-genital organizations (the oral and anal-sadistic organization) and the infantile genital (also called the phallic phase).

Freud initially describes the anal-sadistic organization, in 1913, when publishing the article, *The Disposition to Obsessional Neurosis*, and only in 1915, two years after this publication, he refers to the oral organization, when publishing the third edition of the *Three Essays*. Thus, the notion of anal stage appears prior to the oral stage. In both organizations, the drives are partial and their goals are the satisfaction upon appropriate stimulation of their erogenous zones.

Freud understands the erogenous zone as "a part of the skin or the mucosa where certain types of stimulation cause pleasurable feeling of certain quality"[30]. These dominant erogenous zones are the mouth (in oral phase) and the anus (in anal-sadistic phase); but, in a footnote added to the *Three Essays*, in 1915, Freud stresses that "the use of other observations led me to assign the erotogenic property to all parts of the body and all internal organs"[31]. Freud, when deepening the discussions on the erogenous zones, understands that any point of the skin or the mucosa can take its burden as an erogenous zone. Such a claim is reiterated at the end of his work when he points out that "the most prominent parts of the body that this libido originates are known by the name of 'erogenous zones', although, in fact, the entire body is an erogenous zone of this type"[32].

Violante, in her understanding about the relevance of the pre-genital organizations and its corresponding erogenous zones for the psychic constitution, considers that "all the time Freud refers to the erogenous body, that is, the body that has psychic representation for having being libidinally invested by

---

lity. *ESB*, vol. VII, 1996, p.186.
30 Idem, p.172.
31 Idem, p. 173.
32 FREUD, Sigmund (1940 [1938]). Outline of Psychoanalysis. *ESB*, vol. XXIII, p.176.

the mother, first, and then by the child himself and by others; therefore, he is never talking about a biological body"[33].

The oral phase: the prototype of the first identifications

The first pre-genital organization is the oral (or cannibalistic). For Freud, in this organization, "the sexual activity is not yet separated from nutrition, and it is differentiated from opposing currents inside it"[34]. In this organization there is already the opposition between active and passive. Sexual pleasure is related to buccal excitement and to suction, since, at the beginning of the baby's life, the psychic activity focuses on providing oral zone's needs satisfaction, such as sucking milk from the mother breast and sucking another object that replaces the mother breast, such as the baby bottle. The act of sucking the mother breast is the main activity that provides pleasure to the baby, where his lips behave as an erogenous zone. Thus, sexuality begins to manifest itself shortly after the first satisfaction experience, during and after breastfeeding, when the baby starts sucking the mother breast and, later, a pacifier or finger, and the latter is an autoerotic child sexual manifestation.

For Freud, "the child act that sucks is determined by the search for a pleasure ever experienced and now remembered[35]. The child, due to his first enjoyable experiences strives to repeat them, since sucking the breast (or bottle) might provide him pleasure. In this first phase, the oral eroticism is in the foreground and the satisfaction sought through the erogenous zone of the lip when sucking the breast, thumb and pacifier aims to

33 VIOLANTE, Maria Lucia Vieira. On Psychosexuality. In: *Freudian Essays Around the Psychosexuality*. São Paulo: Via Leterra, 2004, p. 62.

34 Idem, p.187.

35 Idem, p.171.

pursuit the previously experienced pleasure. Therefore, the erogenous oral zone persists throughout the individual life, near the erogenization of other body areas.

According to Freud, in this organization, "the sexual target consists in the incorporation of the object, model that later will play, in the form of identification, an important psychic role"[36]. During the oral phase, the goal is the embodiment and Freud relates that this incorporation is the prototype of the first child identifications.

In 1921, Freud resumes the identificatory issues. He conceptualized that the identification "is the most remote expression of an emotional link with another person"[37]. In this first moment of life, the boy can demonstrate an interest in the father (or who may replace him). This boy would like to be like him and grow like him. The hostility to the father, at this time, is not present yet. At the same time in which the boy shows an identification with the father figure, he can also bear a cathexis of object regarding the mother, according to the anaclitic or binding choice. Therefore, both the identification and the object choice subsist side by side for a certain time, and the Oedipus complex (which will be discussed when addressing the infantile genital organization) originate from these two chains.

When addressing the identification with the psychic constitution, Freud declares that this identification "behaves as a derivative of the first phase of libido organization, the oral phase, in which the object we value and which we desire is assimilated by the ingestion [...]"[38]. Through the identification, the object is assimilated, incorporated or introjected in the ego, since this identification is in close correlation with the oral incorporation.

---

36 Idem, p.187.
37 FREUD, Sigmund (1921). Group Psychology and the Analysis of the Ego. *ESB*, vol. XVIII, 1996, p.115.
38 Idem, ibidem.

When publishing *The Ego and the Id* (1923), Freud postulates that "at first, in the individual primitive oral phase, the object cathexis and the identification are, undoubtedly, indistinguishable from each other [...]. The character of the ego is a precipitate of abandoned object cathexis and which [...] contain the history of these object choices"[39]. In this text, Freud still compares the identification to the introjection mechanism, having them as synonyms. Based on his studies on melancholy (where there is a replacement of object cathexis by the identification), Freud understands that the identification process is very often in the primitive stages of psychic constitution, and the effects of the first identifications is made in the general primitive childhood and lasts during the adulthood.

In his reading about the first identifications in the early psychic constitution in males, Bleichmar understands that "the traits of the male identification are provided through the parental mean even before the anatomical differentiation may take its place [...]. The path of identificatory introjection is the breast: libidinal support of the appropriation exchange with the alike"[40].

On the *New Conferences*, published in 1933, when addressing the oral phase, Freud reiterates that "the erogenous zone of the mouth dominates what can be called the sexual activity from this period of life"[41]; but shortly after, he declares that "this repetition [of oral phase] was necessary, so that I could use it as a starting point for a report of the progresses in our knowledge"[42]. This progress in the psychoanalytic knowledge is related to Karl Abraham thesis on pre-genital phases which focuses on the libido development.

---

39   FREUD, Sigmund (1923). Op. cit. *ESB*, vol. XIX, 1996, p.42.
40   BLEICHMAR, Silvia. *In the Origins of the Psychic Subject: from Myth to History*. Porto Alegre: Artes Médicas, 1993, p.191-192.
41   FREUD, Sigmund (1933 [1932]). XXXII Conference – Anxiety and Instinct Life. ESB, vol. XXII, p. 101.
42   Idem, ibidem.

Thus, in his contributions to Freudian metapsychology, Abraham, this "loyal disciple of Freud"[43], states that:

> We are obliged to admit that there is a differentiation within the oral phase of libido [...]. In the primary level of that phase, the child's libido is linked to the sucking act. This act is the incorporation [...]. Still there is no differentiation between the child that sucks and the breast that feeds. Furthermore, the child has no feelings of hate or love. His mental state is therefore free, at this stage, of all ambivalence manifestations [...]. In the biting stage of the oral phase, the individual incorporates the object in itself and, thus, destroys it [...]. This is the state in which predominate the cannibalistic drives. It is at this stage that the ambivalent attitude of the ego with his object begins to develop[44].

Through his clinical experience with melancholic patients, Abraham proposed to subdivide the oral phase in two stages: the precocious oral phase (the milk suction phase) and the sadistic-oral phase (of biting). The latter corresponds to the appearance of the teeth. In this, the biting and devouring activity implies an object destruction; as the first ambivalent drives towards the incorporated object also begin to emerge.

Freud agrees with Abraham about this subdivision of the oral phase, postulating:

43 ROUDINESCO, E. & PLÓN, M. *Psychoanalysis Dictionary*. Translation of Vera Ribeiro and Lucy Magalhães. Rio de Janeiro: Jorge Zahar, 1998, p.1.

44 ABRAHAM, Karl (1924). Brief Study of the Libido Development Seen in the Light of Mental Disorders. In: *Psychoanalytic Theory of Libido*. Translation of Christiano Monteiro Oiticica. 6th edition. Rio de Janeiro: Imago, 1970, p.112.

We can be proud of having learned a lot of new stuff, especially about the first libido organizations, and we have obtained a clearer understanding of the importance of what is old; and to demonstrate this I will give you at least some examples. Abraham showed, in 1924, that one can distinguish two stages in the sadistic-anal phase […]. Similarly, we are certain to make a similar subdivision in the first phase, the oral phase. In the first stage [the oral], what is in question is only the oral incorporation, there is absolutely no ambivalence in relation to the object - the mother breast. The second stage, characterized by the appearance of the biting activity, can be described as 'oral-sadistic'. This shows, for the first time, the ambivalence phenomena, which become so clear, later, in the anal-sadistic phase[45].

This subdivision in Freud oral phase is maintained until the end of his work, when he says that "during this phase […], indeed sadistic drives sporadically occur, along with the appearance of the teeth"[46]. The master is referring to the sadistic drives of biting and devouring the object (the mother breast) that appear in the oral phase. So, since Abraham, the researches on the psychoanalytic theory of libido advanced with the more contemporary psychoanalysts' studies, such as those of Bion and Winnicott, updating the contributions of this German psychoanalyst to the Freudian metapsychology.

45 FREUD, Sigmund (1933 [1932]).XXXII Conference – Anxiety and Instinct Life. *ESB*, vol. XXII, p. 101-102.
46 FREUD, Sigmund (1940 [1938]). Outline of Psychoanalysis. *ESB*, vol. XXIII, p.166-167.

The anal-sadistic phase: an approach on sadism and anal-eroticism

The second pre-genital phase described by Freud is the anal-sadistic. In this organization, "the instinct components that dominate this pre-genital organization of sexual life are the anal-erotic and sadistic"[47]. In this organization, the active inclination (of domain) is fed by sadism and the passive inclination to anal eroticism.

According to Freud, at this phase, "the division into opposites that pervades the sexual life is already constituted, but they still cannot be called masculine and feminine, but active and passive"[48]. At this stage, the dominant erogenous zone is the anal. The activity is a result of the domination drive (sadism) through the body muscles and the intestine erogenous mucosa of the intestine becomes the organ of the passive sexual target (of anal eroticism). Concomitantly to the retention or expulsion of the feces there are partial drives that act in a self-erotic manner. So, at this stage, the opposite impulsive pairs are already developed, i.e., the ambivalence between active and passive is already present.

Freud emphasizes that the "intestinal catarrhs in the earlier childhood leave the child 'nervous' [...]. In the later neurotic illness, they have a determining influence in the somatic manifestation of neurosis"[49]. The anal erogenous zone preserves, in adult life, a considerable portion of the genital excitability and, in most remote childhood, certain intestinal disorders may have provoked intense excitations. In these disorders, the boy can come to feel pleasure in erogenous stimulation while retain-

47 FREUD, Sigmund (1913). The Inclination to the Obsessional Neurosis: a Contribution to the Problem of the Neurosis Choice. *ESB*, vol. XII, 1996, p. 345.

48 FREUD, Sigmund (1905). Three Essays on the Theory of Sexuality. *ESB*, vol. VII, 1996, p. 187.

49 Idem, p.175.

ing the fecal mass. This retention denotes the manifestation of sadistic drives of the child, providing him the (dis) pleasure.

For Freud "the fecal mass retention [...] is, also, one of the roots of the so frequent constipation in neuropaths"[50]. The so frequent constipation in childhood provides the anal zone stimulation and may be demonstrating the child pertinacity in relation to people who take care of him. And when growing, this game of retaining feces may be symbolically present in the special scatological rituals, in ceremonial acts and similar acts which are carefully kept confidential by the neurotic individual. Thus, these disturbances have a determining influence on neurosis manifestation in adulthood.

In 1908, Freud publishes *Character and Anal Eroticism* and resumes the point of view of the children who feel pleasure in faces retention, postulating: "we deduce from such indications that these people were born with a sexual constitution in which the erogenous character of the anal zone is exceptionally strong [...]".[51]. In the course of psychic development, the excitements from the anal erogenous zone suffer several variations, and a large part of these excitations can be deflected of sexual purposes and directed towards other purposes, and this process is called sublimation. As a result of the anal eroticism sublimation the triad of three characteristics is formed comprising a series of character traits: the orderly (those who fulfill their duties), parsimonious and obstinate people. Both the order, and the parsimony and obstinacy are interlinked with each other.

I consider that these three character traits associated with the sublimation of anal eroticism had been referred to by Freud, in a letter to Jung, dated October 27, 1906, one year after publishing the *Three Essays*. In that, the master, when addressing the infantile sexuality and underlining the pleasure that the feces re-

---

50 Idem, ibidem.
51 FREUD, Sigmund (1908). Character and Anal Eroticism. *ESB*, vol. IX, 1996, p.159.

tention provides to some children, he states that these, in adulthood, "are extremely clean, miser and obstinate, traits that, so to speak, are sublimations of anal eroticism"[52].

In his contributions to the sublimation of anal eroticism, Ernest Jones considers that:

> The psychic energy that accompanies the desires and feelings related to the region [anal] is almost fully diverted to other directions, leading to sublimation and reactive formations that are the subject of this work [...]. It is amazing how many tasks and actions can symbolize the unconscious act of defecation [...]. Much of the intolerant pathologically insistence on the absolute need for doing certain things in the 'right' manner is derived from this source [...]. In all these activities, the desire for perfection becomes visible. Nothing can be done in half [...]. Such people fight for their rights and dignity, and rebel against any authority. As children, they are extremely disobedient [...]. They can, subsequently, develop a reactive formation against this, leading to an unusual gentleness [...]. They become particularly agitated against the idea of something being taken away from them against their will, especially if it is something that symbolizes feces in the unconscious, for example, the money [...]. The concept of time is, because of the sense of value related to it, an unconscious equivalent of the excretory product [...]. The anal-erotic complex is genetically related to two of the more essential and remote instincts, the instincts of possessing and creating [...]. The desire to handle the product and creating something leads to several sublimations, starting with

52 MCGUIRE, William. *Complete Correspondence of Sigmund Freud and Carl G. Jung*. Rio de Janeiro, Imago, p. 48.

the usual preference of children by the modeling and handling of glass mass, clay etc.[53].

In addition to the sublimation of anal eroticism, Freud states that "the intestinal content [...] also has for the breastfeeding other important senses. It is obviously treated as a part of his own body, representing the first 'gift': when disposing of it, the little creature can express docility to the environment surrounding him, and when refusing it, his stubbornness"[54]. During the pre-genital organization, the feces represent the first gift that the child can give someone that he likes, demonstrating his obedience. If he refuses to give his feces (defecating out of the diaper or the pot), this child is expressing his aggression. Therefore, all relationships, in this phase, are impregnated with symbolic meanings linked to feces.

The master states that "the feces are the child first gift, the first sacrifice in the name of his affection, a part of his own body that is ready to share, but only with someone whom he loves"[55]. The act of defecating offers the first opportunity for which the child must choose between a narcissistic attitude and an attitude of object love. This means that or he shares his feces on behalf of his love or he retains it with the autoerotic or aggressiveness satisfaction purpose. The child can use the feces as an expression of defiance, symbolically denoting his hatred; or on the contrary, when ceding the feces, he is expressing his feelings of love. Therefore, the act of giving the feces to whom this child loves is the first moment in which the boy shares a piece of his own body in order to win the favors of anybody else and this act symbolizes, primarily, the narcissistic love transition (if he retained the feces) for the object love.

53 JONES, Ernest (1918). Traits of Anal-Erotic Character. In: *Obsessive Neurosis*. Manoel Tosta Berlinck (org). São Paulo: Escuta, 2005, p. 295-321.

54 FREUD, Sigmund (1908). Character and Anal Eroticism. *ESB*, vol. IX, 1996, p.175-176.

55 FREUD, Sigmund (1918[1914]). History of An Infantile Neurosis. *ESB*, vol. XVII, 1996, p.89.

This ambivalence between love and hate is resumed by Freud, in 1915, when publishing *The Drives and its Vicissitudes*, stating that "in the highest stage of anal-sadistic organization [...], the fight for the object appears in the form of an eagerness to dominate [...]. The love in this preliminary phase is not distinguished from his hate is his attitude towards the object"[56]. During this organization, love and hate can be considered as a pair of ambivalent drives, but Freud notes that "hatred, as a relationship with the objects, is older than love"[57]. This hatred comes from the narcissistic ego repudiation to the outside world. Thus, in anal-sadistic organization, amorous drives are followed by hatred drives towards the same object; and, if there is a regression of libido to anal-sadistic phase, this hatred could be reinforced if there is a breach with the beloved object.

According to Freud, "in unconscious products – spontaneous ideas, fantasies and symptoms –, the concepts of feces [...], baby and evil penis are distinguished from each other and are easily interchangeable"[58]. For the master, as the act of retaining or expelling feces stimulates the intestinal mucous membrane, this 'stick' of feces plays the role of 'anal penis' in relation to this membrane, since this column or stick of feces symbolically represents the 'anal penis' inside the intestine membrane. While retaining and, subsequently, expelling these feces, this movement of coming and going within the intestine membrane can cause pleasure and displeasure sensations. If, on one hand we have those sensations of pleasure or displeasure in the remote childhood, on the other hand, Freud claims that feces, baby and penis are treated as symbolic equivalents, and can replace each other in the formation of the neurotic symptom.

56 FREUD, Sigmund (1915). Op. cit. *ESB*, vol. XIV, 1996, p.143.
57 Idem, ibidem.
58 FREUD, Sigmund (1917). The transformations of Instinct Exemplified in Anal Eroticism. *ESB*, vol. XVII, p. 136.

On this symbolic equivalence, the master postulates that "faeces, penis and baby are three solid bodies; all three forcing penetration or expulsion, and stimulate a membranous passage"[59]. This means that the libidinal cathexis of these three elements can displace or intensify, since they are symbolically equivalent and one replaces the other. In addition, in the remote childhood, due to the fact that the intestine mucous membrane is stimulated by the passage of feces, this stimulation feeds the passive inclination of anal eroticism and, consequently, the homosexual drives. During the anal eroticism organization, a fortification of anal eroticism allows an inclination to homosexuality when the genitals organs primacy is achieved.

In his book *Psychoanalytic Theory of Neurosis*, Otto Fenichel understands that "anal eroticism is always of bisexual character: the anus is, at the same time, the organ that actively expels and a hollow organ, possible to be stimulated by any object that enters it […]".[60].

In addition to the anal eroticism fortification, which can leave a great inclination to homosexuality, Freud states that the "old interest for the feces becomes the great value granted to gold and money […]"[61]. The interest for the money is taken from the anal-erotic sources, since the commitment on defecation disappears in later stages of adulthood, becoming the value granted to gold and money. Thus, the interest for the money enables the transfer of early drive to this new object.

The first associations between money and feces are already present in the early days of psychoanalysis, when writing to Fliess, Freud associates money and avarice with feces, as says: "I can hardly enumerate to you the things that I can transform into excrement. This fits perfectly to the theory of internal bad

59 Idem, p. 141.
60 FENICHEL, Otto. Op. cit. São Paulo: Atheneu, 1981, p.259.
61 FREUD, Sigmund (1933[1932]). XXXII Conference – Anxiety and Instinct Life. *ESB*, vol. XXII, 1996, p.103.

smell [...]. I think that the association [of money] is made from the word 'dirty' as a synonym for 'miser' [...]"[62].

In his contributions to the relation between money and the anal-sadistic phase, the German physician and psychoanalyst Karl Abraham says:

> These people social behavior [anal-erotic] are strongly connected to the money [...]. They [...] tend to become patrons of the arts or benefactors of any kind [...]. Their special attitude towards money [...] is usually an attitude of parsimony or avarice [...]. There are cases in which the relationship between the feces intentional retention and the systematic parsimony is perfectly clear [...] while in other aspects they spend money with a surprising liberality [...]. The avarice, money, or money value displacement to time can be often observed [...]. The pleasure in regulating the work through regular schedules is well known as constitution an expression of anal character[63].

Abraham also brings another huge contribution to the anal-sadistic phase understanding, subdividing it into two levels, and so:

> The psychoanalytic experience has forced us to state the existence of a pre-genital phase of libidinal development [anal phase] and we are currently taken to assume that this phase contains, in itself, two different levels. In the subsequent level, conservative inclinations prevail to re-

62 FREUD, Sigmund (1897). Letter of December 22, 1897. *ESB*, vol. I, p. 324.

63 ABRAHAM, Karl (1921). Contributions to the Theory of Anal Character. In: *Psychoanalytic Theory of Libido*. Translation of Christiano Monteiro Oiticica. 6th edition. Rio de Janeiro: Imago, 1970, p. 184-188.

tain and control the object, whereas in the older level, the hostile inclinations to the object – to destroy it and lose it – come to the foreground […]. This differentiation of the sadistic-anal phase in a primitive stage and another posterior appears to have a radical importance because the dividing line between these two phases provides a decisive change in the individual attitude towards the outside world[64].

In the *New Conferences*, published in 1932/1933, Freud incorporates this contribution of Abraham to his theory, as he says: "we can be proud of having learned a lot of new things, especially about the first libido organizations [...]. Abraham showed, in 1924, that one can distinguish two stages in the sadistic-anal phase"[65]. The master is referring to the subdivision of anal-sadistic phase. The first of these stages is dominated by inclinations for destroying and losing, and the second stage by affectionate inclinations towards the objects (like the inclinations to maintain and possess)[66].

According to Freud, the amplitude of sadistic drives "is much higher in the second phase [anal-sadistic], since this is the so sought satisfaction in aggression and in the excretory function"[67]. At this phase, the sadism is constituted by the drive fusion of purely libidinal (Eros) and destructive (Thanatos) drives.

64   ABRAHAM, Karl (1924). Brief Study of the Libido Development Seen in the Light of Mental Disorders. In: *Psychoanalytic Theory of Libido*. Translation of Christiano Monteiro Oiticica. 6th edition. Rio de Janeiro: Imago, 1970, p. 94.

65 FREUD, Sigmund (1933 [1932]).XXXII Conference – Anxiety and Instinct Life. *ESB*, vol. XXII, p. 101.

66 Remember that Abraham assigns this second inclination to obsessive neurosis and the first to melancholy.

67 FREUD, Sigmund (1940[1938]). Outline of Psychoanalysis. *ESB,* vol. XXIII, p. 167.

The infantile genital organization: the phallic phase

In an added footnote, in 1924, to the *Three Essays*, Freud says that "[...] after the two pre-genital organizations, there is a third phase in child development: this, which already deserves the name of genital [...] only knows one type of genitalia: the male. That is why I called it the phallic stage of organization"[68]. This third organization described by Freud is the infantile genital organization. Due to the primacy of the phallus (and not the penis), this organization is also named by Freud as phallic phase. At this point, the early childhood sexuality reaches its peak. During this phase the Oedipus complex and the castration complex culminate and articulate – both, at this time, reach their culminating point and which resolution should occur by the end of childhood.

Freud postulates that the infantile genital organization "consists in the fact that, for both genders, only one genital organ is considered, namely, the male"[69]. At this phase of phallus primacy, both the boys and the girls only recognize one genital organ: the male. In the case of the boy, this occupies his interest since he feels pleasure in this part of the body and he thinks that all people have it. Therefore, the infantile sexual curiosities purpose is to compare who has the male genital organ – phallic – and who does not have it – castrated.

For a further understanding of these curiosities, I would like to make a little digression on the sexual theories. In 1907, when publishing the article, The Sexual Enlightenment of Children, Freud postulates that "it would be worth to collect and examine such infantile sexual theories [...]"[70]. At this time, Freud was supervising the analysis of little Hans, performed by his father. In this article, Freud brings small excerpts from this case,

68 FREUD, Sigmund (1905). Three Essays on the Theory of Sexuality. *ESB*, vol. VII, 1996, p.188.
69 FREUD, Sigmund (1923). The Infantile Genital Organization: An Interpolation on the Theory of Sexuality. *ESB*, vol. XIX, 1996, p.158.
70 FREUD, Sigmund (1907). Op. cit. *ESB*, vol. IX, 1996, p.128.

highlighting the sexual curiosities of this child. Let us remember that little Hans asked the parents, including the mother, if she also had a 'pee-pee'. So, at this point, Freud develops a brief examination of infantile sexual fantasies, that is, "the infantile sexual theories", which allows understanding the anatomical sexual difference for children.

It is in the article *On the Sexual Theories of Children* (published in 1908), that the master states that "the first of these theories derives from the ignorance of the differences between the genders [...]. This is to assign to all, including women, the possession of a penis, such as the boy knows from his own body"[71]. At this stage in the development of his theory, Freud had not yet specifically addressed the phallic phase (which would only occur in 1923) and its interlinking with the Oedipus complex and the castration complex (which would occur in 1925); but he already points out that the penis becomes the primary erogenous zone to the child at this time of his psychosexual development and, for the boy, his most important self-erotic sexual object.

For the boy, according to Freud, it could have occurred that, during the masturbation act, "his parents and his babysitter surprised him in that act and intimidated him with the threat to cut off his penis. The effect of this 'threat of castration' is proportional to the value given to the organ [...]"[72]. The boy, instantly, does not believe in the threat made by the parents or does not obey it absolutely. In this phase, the masturbatory activity is very frequent as a manner to provide pleasure. The boy is used to get pleasure by stimulating this genital organ with his hand and he is unable to think of a person like him devoid of this organ; but, when seeing the genitals of a little friend or sister, he can imagine that this could grow when she grows up (remember the little Hans when seeing his little sister showering) or this child can distort this perception, denying it.

---

71 FREUD, Sigmund (1908). Op. cit. *ESB*, vol. IX, 1996, p.196.
72 Idem, p.197.

In addition to these possible observations in remote childhood, we cannot forget that, among the elaborations of the infantile sexual theories, we have the concept of primary scene. For the master:

> "the childhood early scenes [...] are not reproductions of real occurrences [...]. I consider them, before, as products of the imagination [...] which indent to serve as a kind of symbolic representation of true desires and interests and that may be originated in a regressive inclination"[73].

The primary scene can be interpreted, within the infantile sexual theories, as an anal intercourse. This scene is linked to sexual intercourse between parents that may have been observed or supposedly dreamed by the child, being interpreted as a violent and sadistic act, by the father.

According to Freud, these "scenes [...] that date from a premature period and exhibit a similar content [...] have to be [...] gradually and laboriously constructed from a set of indications"[74]. The analyst understands this scene through the constructions permeated by the dreams associations of his patients[75]. This means that the interpretation of all the dream formations may lead back to this scene. Remember the primary scene of the Wolf Man and his respective child dream with the six or seven wolves, which caused so much anxiety. Therefore, the primary scene represents the sexual intercourse – *a coitus a tergo* – between the parents, which may have been seen or fantasized by the child, being this scene interpreted as part of an infantile sexual theory.

---

73 FREUD, Sigmund (1918[1914]). History of An Infantile Neurosis. *ESB*, vol. XVII, 1996, p.60.

74 Idem, p. 61-62.

75 These constructions have occurred in the analysis of the clinical case of this thesis, providing a unique understanding on the sadistic fantasies present in the remote childhood of Paulo.

Mijolla-Mellor, in her understanding of the primitive scene (or origin scene), understands this as:

> "the sexual intercourse scene between parents, observed, constructed, fantasized by the child and interpreted by him in terms of violence [...]. The notion of 'origin scene" only appears in Freud in 1918 due to the Wolf Man [...]. The fantasy of the origin scene, similar to infantile sexual theories, has a typical character, and is present in all the neurotics, or better, in all human beings [...]. Freud also insisted on the 'reality' of the scene, reopening the debate between 'objective reality' and 'psychic reality'. However, beyond the scene itself, it is the entire issue of fantasy that is raised [...]. Many of the real scenes are not accessible by reminiscence; they are only remembered by the dream [...]. The original scene is inseparable of the infantile sexual theories, which formation he raises [...] "[76].

In addition to the primary scene being one of the manifestations of infantile sexual theories framework, the master also points out the importance of sexual research in remote childhood.

According to Freud, "in the course of these researches, the child so discoveries that the penis is not a possession that is common to all creatures that resemble him"[77]. In the course of his sexual researches, the boy comes across with the discovery that the penis is not present in all people. The observation of the female genitals provides the occasion for this discovery, causing the search for explanations for this fact. In addition, at the beginning of the infantile genital organization, having the phallic

---

76 MIJOLLA, Alain de. *International Dictionary of Psychoanalysis*. Translation of Álvaro Cabral. Rio de Janeiro: Imago, 2005, p. 316-317.

77 FREUD, Sigmund (1923). The Infantile Genital Organization: An Interpolation on the Theory of Sexuality. *ESB*, vol. XIX, 1996, p.159.

mother as an object of his incestuous desire, the boy has his perception and fantasies respond to his enigmas about the babies' birth, their origin, their sexuality and sexual difference.

According to Freud, "the antithesis here is between having a male genital organ or being castrated"[78]. That is, having the phallus or being castrated and this antithesis (preceded by the opposition between active and passive of the anal-sadistic phase) is present on the Oedipus complex, which is now articulated with the castration complex.

The Oedipus complex and the castration complex.

In an added footnote, in 1920, to the *Three Essays*, Freud says:

> It has been stated [...] that the Oedipus complex is the nuclear complex of neurosis [...]. In it the infantile sexuality is culminated, which, by its aftereffects, decisively influences the adult sexuality. Every new human being faces the task of dominating the Oedipus complex, and the one that cannot do it succumbs to the neurosis[79].

Therefore, the Oedipus complex can be considered the nuclear complex of the psychic subject constitution and the consequences of his repression determine neurosis later in adult life.

When publishing *The Ego and the Id*, in 1923, Freud resumes the discussion on this complex, stating that "an ambivalent attitude towards the father and an object-type relationship only affectionate with the mother are the contents of the Oedipus complex in the boy"[80]. Both the father and the mother are

---

78 Idem, p.161.
79 FREUD, Sigmund (1905). Three Essays on the Theory of Sexuality. *ESB*, vol. VII, 1996, p.214.
80 FREUD, Sigmund (1923). Op. cit. *ESB*, vol. XIX, 1996, p.44-

present since the beginning of the psychic constitution. The two relationships with these figures (the love to the mother and the hostility to the father) go hand-in-hand, until the child's wishes by this mother become more intense and the father becomes an obstacle to its realization. From the convergence of these two streams the oedipean complex is originated in its simple form. In this, the hostility towards the father becomes a desire to get rid of him in order to take his place next to the mother, but Freud states that:

> [...] One gets the impression that the simple Oedipus complex is its most common form, but rather represents a simplification or diagram that is, no doubt, often justified for practical purposes. A deeper study usually reveals the most complete Oedipus complex, which is duplicitous, positive and negative, due to the bisexuality originally present in the child [...]. The analytical experience shows that, in a number of cases, one or another of the constituents disappears, except for barely distinguishable traits; the result, then, is a series with the normal positive Oedipus complex on one end and the reverse negative on the other, while its intermediate members exhibit the full form, with one or other of its two components preponderating[81].

During the infantile genital organization, there is not only the positive Oedipus complex, but concomitantly to this the positive Oedipus complex occurs. This means that a complete Oedipus complex occurs, which is negative and positive, due to the bisexuality originally present in the child. This means that the boy does not present an ambivalent attitude towards his father and an object relation of unique affectionate type with his

45.
81 Idem, p.45-46.

mother. This boy can also behave like a girl and show a female affectionate attitude towards the father and a corresponding jealousy and hostility towards the mother figure.

For Freud, "the Oedipus complex provided the child two possibilities of satisfaction, one active and another passive"[82]. The boy can put himself in the place of the father and seek relationships with the mother, and this possibility is representative of an active satisfaction; or, in the passive possibility, the boy wants to take the mom's place and seeks be loved by the father.

Regarding this passive position before the father figure, we remember the homosexual desire of the Wolf Man: "of being born from the father [...], the desire to be sexually satisfied by his father, the desire to present him with a child [...]"[83]. These desires of Sergei Pankejeff are linked to a necessary condition to get sexual satisfaction from his father, of being copulated by him and to give him a son, and these desires are representatives of the homosexual fantasy of this patient.

Again Freud approaches the desire of giving a son to the father, in the last months of 1922, when writing *A Demonic Neurosis of the 17th Century* and publishing it in 1923. The master, while analyzing the original manuscript of the Bavarian painter Christoph Haizmann, and focusing on him, the mourning for the lost father, he points out that "the thing against which he is rebelling is his female attitude towards the father, which culminates by the fantasy of giving him a son"[84].

In her interpretation of this context in Freudian theory, Violante states that: "Freud no longer reported to this fantasy of the boy in the rest of his work, according to my reading. Thus,

---

82 FREUD, Sigmund (1924). The Dissolution of the Oedipus Complex. *ESB*, vol. XIX, 1996, p.196.

83 FREUD, Sigmund (1918 [1914]). History of An Infantile Neurosis. *ESB*, vol. XVII, 1996, p.109.

84 FREUD, Sigmund (1923[1922]). A Demonic Neurosis of the 17th Century. *ESB*, vol. XIX, 1996, p. 105.

even though, he deals with the fantasy of man being copulated by the father, in the case of the Wolf Man [...]. Instead it appears as a defense the 'repudiation of femininity' – common to the boy and girl, but in him it is expressed by the forceful repression to the passive or female attitude towards another man"[85].

Concomitantly to the search of the two possibilities of satisfaction (the active and the passive), during the Oedipus complex, Freud points out that "the meaning of the castration complex can only be properly appreciated if its origin in the phallic primacy phase is also taken into account"[86]. Articulated to the Oedipus complex, the castration complex performs the interdictory function of the incestuous and parricide desire. So, this complex puts an end to the two possible ways of obtaining satisfaction during the phallic phase. This finds its unit in the phallus – target of symbolic castration (and not the penis).

For Freud, "the lack of a penis [in the girls] is seen as a result of castration and, now, the child faces the task of coming to terms with castration in relation to himself"[87]. When playing, when looking at the genitals of a classmate or his sister, this observation awakens in this boy the suspicion that there is something different. At first, the boy can even reject it and think that the penis was there; but slowly he concludes that the penis was there and was withdrawn.

According to Freud, "only later, when possessed of any threat of castration, the observation becomes important to him; if this is remembered or repeated, it awakens in him a terrible storm of emotion and enforces him to believe in the reality of the threat that he had laughed at so far"[88]. The threat of losing

---

85 VIOLANTE, Maria Lúcia Vieira. *From the "Enigma of woman" to the enigma of man.* Unpublished Text. 2010, p.1-2.

86 FREUD, Sigmund (1923). The Infantile Genital Organization: An Interpolation on the Theory of Sexuality. *ESB*, vol. XIX, 1996, p.159-160.

87 Idem, p.159.

88 FREUD, Sigmund (1925). Some Psychic Consequences of Anato-

his penis gains strength every time he recalls the appearance of the female genitals. Therefore, the dissolution of the Oedipus complex in the boy is caused by the anxiety of castration. At this time, the boy faces the task of coming to terms with castration in relation to himself.

Regarding this dissolution, Freud says:

> If the satisfaction of love in the Oedipus complex field should cost the penis to the child, there might arise a conflict between his narcissistic interest in that part of his body and the libidinal cathexis of his parental objects. In this conflict, usually the first of these forces triumphs: the child ego turns its back to the Oedipus complex[89].

This means that the anxiety of castration – regarding the ghost of narcissistic integrity threat of the penis possession – puts an end to the two possible ways of obtaining the Oedipus complex satisfaction. In order to preserve his sexual organ, the boy must give up the incestuous desire addressed to the mother, due to the fear of the castration ghost to be held by the father as a punishment.

In 1925, when writing *Inhibitions, Symptoms and Anxiety*, Freud says that "it was anxiety that produced the repression and not, as I previously believed, the repression that had produced anxiety"[90]. At this point, he introduces the second theory of anxiety, changing the relationship of anxiety with repression: instead of anxiety resulting from repression, now anxiety leads the ego to the repression. About anxiety, Freud points out that:

---

mical Distinction Between the Sexes. *ESB*, vol. XIX, 1996, p. 281.

89   FREUD, Sigmund (1924). The Dissolution of the Oedipus Complex. *ESB*, vol. XIX, 1996, p.196.

90   FREUD, Sigmund (1926 [1925]). Inhibitions, Symptoms and Anxiety. *ESB*, vol. XX, 1996, p.111.

For each stage of the subject development is reserved, as being suitable for this development, a special determinant factor of anxiety. The danger of psychic helplessness is adjusted to the ego initial immaturity stage; the danger of an object loss (or loss of love) is adjusted to the lack of self-sufficiency of the first years of childhood; the danger of being castrated is adjusted to the phallic phase; and, finally, the fear of the superego, which assumes a special position, is adjusted to the latency period[91].

Every stage of physical development corresponds to a factor of anxiety. During the phallic phase, the driving force of anxiety in the boy is the fear of castration. Thus, the anxiety of castration leads the boy to abandon the incestuous desire regarding the mother but also the desire to eliminate the father. This complex marks the terminal crisis of Oedipus, sealing the prohibition of incest and establishing the role of law: at this time starts, for the boy, the latency period.

Freud, when addressing the Oedipus complex demolition and its repression, says: "I see no reason to deny the name of 'repression' to the ego's distance from the Oedipus complex, although the subsequent repressions occur mostly with the superego participation [...]"[92]. In the boy, due to the anxiety of castration, the infantile sexuality is repressed, and an abolishment, a destruction of this complex occurs, which puts the boy in the latency period. If, on one hand, there is a repression of infantile sexuality, on the other hand, this complex may persist in unconscious state and express its psychopathologic consequences throughout adult life.

---

91 FREUD, Sigmund (1933 [1932]). XXXII Conference – Anxiety and Instinct Life. *ESB*, vol. XXII, 1996, p.91-92.
92 FREUD, Sigmund (1924). The Dissolution of the Oedipus Complex. *ESB*, vol. XIX, 1996, p.196.

In their reading about the castration complex, Laplanche and Pontalis interpreted that this is a:

> Complex centered on the castration fantasy that provides a response to the enigma that the genders anatomical difference (presence or absence of penis) causes to the child [...]. The castration complex is in close relationship with the Oedipus complex and, more specifically, with the interdictory and normative function [...]. In the boy it marks the terminal crisis of Oedipus, and may interdict to the child the maternal object; the anxiety of castration opens for him the latency period and precipitates the superego formation [...] [93].

Beyond the understanding of Laplanche and Pontalis about the castration complex and its intrinsic relationship with the Oedipus complex, another interpretation on the role played by parents throughout this complex is that of the psychoanalyst Silvia Bleichmar, and for her

> the mother crossed by the recognition of castration is in a different position of the origin mother in relation to the boy [a phallic mother]. Between one and another there was this 'affective storm' that Freud described in multiple texts written from 1919. The object varied, their status has changed, there is no direct continuity but a discontinuity marked by ambivalence and by the intervention of another variable that, having been present since the beginning of life, it does not have a meaning until that time for both the girl and the boy: the sexed father [...]. How does the father enter in these times of origins, in which the originally buried in the unconscious is about to be constituted?

93 LAPLANCHE, J. & PONTALIS, J-B (1967). *Vocabulary of Psychoanalysis*. São Paulo: Martins Fontes, 2001, p. 73-74.

> This occurs both in the girl and in the boy, in two different manners: on one hand, as the one that separates the fusion link with the mother [...]; on the other hand, and from the early cares shared, as metonymy of the mother that registers, in turn, remains of perception that are not fully assimilated by the drive moves she exercises [...][94].

Bleichmar understands that the father interdiction in the son, in the strict sense, falls on his Oedipus complex, that is, on the desire towards to the mother as an incest object. In this meander, the change from a passive to an active position is provided by the discovery of female castration, throwing the boy to a narcissistic fall of the maternal object, a fall that carries the castration anxiety of the boy himself and opens the movement that launches him from the identification to the love object choice.

The identifications and the choice of the love object

For a better understanding of movement that leads the boy to the identificatory process and the loving object choice, I would like to make a brief return to the beginning of the 20s. In the wise understanding of Violante about this moment in the Freudian theory, she points out that:

> While achieving a less pathological and more structuring concept of narcissism – unifying both the pre-genital drives which will be under the phallus primacy, and the first manner in which the ego is constituted, being narcissistically invested [...], Freud resumes the concept of identification, left loose, to deal with the ego constitution[95].

---

94 BLEICHMAR, Silvia. *In the Origins of the Psychic Subject: from Myth to History*. Porto Alegre: Artes Médicas, 1993, p.187- 189.

95 VIOLANTE, Maria Lucia Vieira. Narcissism and identification.

When writing about the identification, in *Group Psychology and the Analysis of the Ego*, in 1921, Freud postulates three types of identification. Regarding the first, the master states that the "identification is known [...] as the most remote expression of an emotional link with another person [...]. The first type of link, therefore, is already possible before any sexual object choice has been made"[96]. The first mode is an originary form of affective link with the object and occurs before the Oedipus complex is complete. In this case, the boy can identify himself with his father, and at this time he would like to be like his father, to grow up like him, to be him and take his place in everything. His father becomes his ideal and this identification is not linked to the passive or feminine attitude in relation to this referential figure, because this identification is before the oedipean rivalry – being related to the object incorporation according to the cannibalistic model (as already mentioned in the oral phase).

In the second mode, Freud postulates that "the identification appeared in the place of object choice and the object choice has regressed to the identification"[97]. This succeeds the dissolution of Oedipus complex. This is recognized as regressive identification, i.e. where the repression occurred and the unconscious mechanisms are dominant, the object choice retroacts for the identification and the ego acquires the object characteristics, such as the hysterical symptom, which can represent the identification resulting from the Oedipus complex. The child does not imitate the person, but rather, the loved person symptom – just like Dora that imitated her father cough.

In the third mode, Freud states that "the identification leaves any object relationship with the person being copied ful-

In: *Freudian Essays Around the Psychosexuality*. São Paulo: via Leterra, 2004, p. 79-80.

96 FREUD, Sigmund (1921). Group Psychology and the Analysis of the Ego. *ESB*, vol. XVIII, 1996, p.115 -116.

97 Idem, p.116.

ly out of consideration"[98]. In this mode occurs identification to a trait of another individual, by which the boy seeks to imitate him. The subject can identify himself with another person to the extent that both have an element in common, although this identification is performed in the absence of any libidinal investment.

Mezan, while highlighting the three identificatory modes mentioned in the text *Group Psychology and the Analysis of the Ego* (1921), understands that:

> In all these cases, the identification is translated into a modification in the ego, in the form of residue or deposit; the ego is constituted by these successive identifications, which may be contradictory and heteroclite. Therefore, as in all cases, the one with whom the subject is identified is outside him, the identification is equivalent to an opening operation to the external reality, consisting of strange factors to the individual purely impulsive life [...]. If we return to the excerpt of Collective Psychology in which Freud introduces the concept of identification, we see that the Oedipus complex is the topic that drives his reasoning [...][99].

In *The Ego and the Id* (1923), again Freud addresses the identificatory process, linking this with the development of the ego. He states that "when a person has to abandon a sexual object, very often there is a change of his ego that can only be described as object installation within the ego [...]"[100]. After drawing comments on melancholy (in which the melancholic subject

98 FREUD, Sigmund (1921). Group Psychology and the Analysis of the Ego. *ESB*, vol. XVIII, 1996, p.117.

99 MEZAN, Renato (1985). *Freud, Thinker of Culture*. 7th edition. São Paulo: Companhia das Letras, 2006, p. 506-507.

100 FREUD, Sigmund (1923). The Ego and the Id. *ESB*, vol. XIX, 1996, p.42.

identifies with the lost object), Freud discusses the identification as a synonym of introjection, where there is a replacement of the object cathexis by the identification.

In the same article, Freud says that "may be, through this introjection, which consists of a kind of regression to the oral phase mechanism, the ego makes it easier to the object to be abandoned or make this process possible"[101]. Remember that the identification occurs in the primitive stages of development, allowing understanding, according to Freud, that the ego character is a precipitate of abandoned object cathexis and this ego contains the history of these choices. But Freud points out that "[...] the object choices belong to the first sexual period and are related to the father and to the mother they usually find its outcome in an identification of this kind, which would strengthen the primary"[102]. I understand that Freud is linking the notion of identification to the Oedipus complex, since he is referring to the subsequent identification to the oedipean resolution that may consummate the primary identification – an identification in which the object is assimilated by the ingestion and incorporated into the ego.

In the reading of Laplanche and Pontalis, the primary identification

> is in close correlation with the so-called oral incorporation ratio [...]. The primary identification is opposed to secondary identifications that may overlap it, not only to the extent in which it is the first chronologically, but also to the extent in which an actual object relationship would not have been consecutively established [...]. It is interesting to note that Freud, which only rarely uses the

---

101 Idem, ibidem.
102 FREUD, Sigmund (1923). The Ego and the Id. *ESB*, vol. XIX, 1996, p.44.

term primary identification [...] thus assigns an identification with the father of the 'personal prehistory', taken by the boy as ideal or prototype [...]. This would be a direct and immediate identification which occurs prior to any object investment[103].

According to Freud, "in the dissolution of the Oedipus complex, the four trends in which he consists will group in order to produce a paternal identification and a maternal identification"[104]. In the case of the boy, after the oedipean resolution, the object cathexis are abandoned and replaced by identifications. These identifications were already present in his ego during the pre-genital and infantile genital organizations. The place of the former maternal cathexis can be filled by an identification with the mother, such as the old place of paternal cathexis, which can be filled by an intensification of his identification with the father figure, and this is the most common result in neuroses field, which allows that the affectionate relationship with the mother is preserved and confirms the manhood in the case of the boy. This identification with the father preserves the object relationship with the mother (belonging to the positive complex) and replaces the object relationship with the father (belonging to the negative complex). And during the psychic development, the father place may be occupied by teachers and other people placed in position of authority. Consequently, the identifications, having as a model the parental figures, are repeated, later, in the boy adult life.

When publishing the *New Conferences* (1932/1933), Freud defines identification as "the action of resembling an ego to another ego, as a consequence that the first ego behaves like the second in certain aspects, imitates it and, in a sense, assim-

103 LAPLANCHE, J. & PONTALIS, J-B (1967). *Vocabulary of Psychoanalysis* . São Paulo: Martins Fontes, 2001, p. 231-232.
104 FREUD, Sigmund (1923). The Ego and the Id. *ESB*, vol. XIX, 1996, p.46.

ilates it inside itself"[105]. At this point of his work, unlike the notions of incorporation and introjection, Freud considers the identification as an action of an ego resembling to another ego. This ego, which seeks the identification, behaves with the identified ego, imitating it and assimilating it within its ego. Thus, the identification is a very important manner of linking to someone else, and this is different from the object choice.

Freud states that "identification and object choice are, in a large extent, independent of one another"[106]. If the boy may identify himself with the father, he wants to be equal to this model and his ego changes according to this model; but, if the boy has the father as an object of his choice, he wants to have him. In this case, the boy identifies with his mother and has his father as the object of choice. This kind of narcissistic choice of object is common in cases of male homosexuality.

In his understanding of the identificatory process, Mezan states that identification:

> is a process through which the subject assimilates one or more traits of another individual, integrating them to his ego and therefore changes according to the model or models in question. It is different [...] from the object choice, to the extent that choosing an object is wishing to have it, while identifying to an object is wanting to be it or being as it is [...][107].

In another reading on the identificatory process and the rise to manhood, Bleichmar says:

---

105 FREUD, Sigmund (1933 [1932]). XXXI Conference: The Dissection of the Psychic Personality. *ESB*, vol. XXII, 1996, p. 68.
106 Idem, p. 69.
107 MEZAN, Renato (1985). *Freud, Thinker of Culture*. 7th edition. São Paulo: Companhia das Letras, 2006, p. 506.

We know the paradox of male identification: being like the father – while possessing the mother. However, how could an identification to a pure rival, a pure obstacle, occur without a love link with him? [...]. The fact that every identification refers to an introjection, and this to a symbolic appropriation mode, no doubt, but ultimately the phantasmal object from which the other is carrier, proposes us the highly conflicting character of male sexuality constitution [...]. How could the son receive the father's penis that makes him sexually potent if it was not from its incorporation? Introjective incorporation that leaves masculinity forever handed over to the paradoxical ghost of homosexuality [...][108].

In the understanding Bleichmar, the incorporation of the paternal sadist penis launches a new look towards the ghost of homosexuality present in male identificatory issue, since, if passivity, which is really repressed in man, and the homosexuality, it would be convenient to search the two sides that constitutes it as structural, and not as bisexual waste of some phantasmal biology

For this psychoanalyst, these two aspects would be from the passive position of the boy in his remote childhood and the consequences of phantasmal incorporation of the paternal sadistic penis. This means that, being passive in the early periods of life by his phallic-seducing mother, the boy cannot reach to manhood, but through the phantasmal incorporation of the paternal penis that may offer its articulating power while anally subjecting in the exchanges that establishes the circuit his masculinization. With that explained, I would like to return to the Freudian work.

---

108 BLEICHMAR, Silvia. *In the Origins of the Psychic Subject: from Myth to History*. Porto Alegre: Artes Médicas, 1993, p. 190-192.

About the identification, Freud also recognizes: "I my-self am not, by no means, satisfied with these comments on iden-tification; but this will be enough if you can ensure me that the installation of the superego can be classified as a successful exam-ple of identification with the parental instance"[109]. Therefore, at this point, this book will give a special emphasis to this psychic instance: the superego.

The superego

The emergence of this higher instance within the ego is closely linked to the destination of the Oedipus complex – giv-en that the superego is the heir of this so important emotional binding in early childhood. Therefore, in a boy, in addition to occurring a possible parental (or maternal) identification, after the repression of his infantile sexuality, the superego and the ide-al of ego are the heirs of the Oedipus complex.

So, starting from the Freudian assertion that the instal-lation of superego can be understood as a successful example of identification with the parental instance, I believe that a thor-ough reading of this critical instance formation is of extreme relevance for understanding the identificatory process in the case of male psychic constitution. And, to address the superego, it is necessary to resume the concept of ideal of ego and its relevant development in Freudian theory. For that, I would like to go to the text of 1914, titled *On Narcissism*: *An Introduction*.

In this text, Freud states that "for the ego, the formation of an ideal would be a conditioning factor of repression"[110]. For the master, the ideal ego – an ego previously invested by his par-ents and then narcissistically by the individual – is the target of the child love and all his narcissism appear shifted toward this

109 FREUD, Sigmund (1933 [1932]). XXXI Conference: The Dis-section of the Psychic Personality. *ESB*, vol. XXII, 1996, p. 69.
110 FREUD, Sigmund (1914). Op. cit. *ESB*, vol. XIV, 1996, p. 100.

instance, which, according to Freud, "is possessed of all perfection of value"[111]. For Freud:

> The man is shown unable to give up a satisfaction that he once enjoyed. He is not willing to give up the narcissistic perfection of his childhood; and when growing up, he is seen disturbed by third parties' admonitions and by the awakening of his own critical judgement, so he is no longer able to retain that perfection, and seeks to recover it under the new form of an ideal of ego. What he projects towards himself as being his ideal is the replacement for the narcissism lost in his childhood in which he was his own ideal[112].

In Freudian metapsychology, the ideal ego and ideal of ego concepts are not mixed up. While the ideal ego can be considered as the love object of infantile narcissism, the ideal of ego is the object of the ego pursuit, a result of the castration assumption effect. So, in the excerpt quoted above, the critical judgement and the ideal of ego are not mixed, since this judgement is prior to the ideal of ego formation.

About the difference between the critical judgement and ideal of ego, Violante understands that "the critical judgement seems to predate the ideal of ego formation through the restriction imposed to the intention of the current ego remaining identified as the ideal ego. This concept is lost on Freudian texts until it is retrieved in 1932/1933, in the 31st conferences of the 'New Conferences...', [...] when Freud assigns to superego the function of being the bearer of the ideal of ego" [113].

---

111 Idem, ibidem.

112 Idem, p. 100-101.

113 VIOLANTE, Maria Lucia Vieira. The Heirs of the Oedipus Complex. In: *Freudian Essays Around the Psychosexuality*. São Paulo: via Leterra, 2004, p. 125-126.

According to Freud, "we would not be surprised if we found a special psychic agent that accomplished the task of ensuring the narcissistic satisfaction from the ideal of ego, and which, with this purpose in view, constantly observed the real ego, measuring it for that ideal"[114]. Freud, when questioning the manner in which the individual could ensure the narcissistic satisfaction from the ideal of ego, assigns this task to an instance called 'our consciousness' or 'censure agent'.

In a footnote added to this paragraph, the English editor James Strachey points out that "it was from combination between this agent and the ideal of ego that Freud later deduced the superego"[115].

In this context, Freud points out that "what induced the individual to form an ideal of ego, on behalf of which his consciousness acts as a surveillance, emerged from the critical influence of his parents (transmitted to him through the voice)"[116]. Subsequently, this critical influence is performed by educators, and also by other people in the environment where the child is inserted to. And in addition to imposing harsh conditions to the satisfaction of libido, Freud also postulates that this ideal, "in addition to its individual aspect, this [...] has its social aspect; also constitutes the common ideal of a family, a class or a nation"[117]. This means that the ideal of ego covers the social aspects of the family group where the child is inserted to.

After mentioning this social aspect of the ideal of ego, Freud considers, in 1917, that "there really is in ego an instance that incessantly observes, criticizes and compares [...]. We know the self-observing instance as a censor of the ego"[118]. In this con-

---

114 FREUD, Sigmund (1914). On Narcissism: An Introduction. *ESB*, vol. XV, 1996, p. 102.

115 Idem, ibidem.

116 Idem, ibidem.

117 Idem, p. 108.

118 FREUD, Sigmund (1917 [1916-1917]). XXVI Conference - The

ference, starting from the understanding of the delirium of observation, Freud is referring to the superego, since this instance exercises the censorship during dreams and from this comes the repressions to the forbidden desires. And he adds: "when [...] this censor instance is broken into its parts, it reveals its origin in the parents, educators and social environment influence in an identification with some of these model figures"[119].

With the publishing of *Mourning and Melancholy*, in 1917, Freud resumes the idea of 'censor instance', 'critical instance'. When analyzing the disturbance of the melancholic, Freud ponders: "we see how part of the ego arises in him against the other, judges him critically, and, so to speak, takes this as its object"[120]. He names this part as 'conscience' and includes it, along with the censorship, among the main functions or superego.

In the understanding of Violante about this excerpt, she considers that, "in Mourning and Melancholia' [...], Freud refers to this 'critical agent' or 'conscience' as a center of conflict in relation to the ego, then regressively identified with the lost object" [121].

Four years after *Mourning and Melancholy*, when publishing *Group Psychology and the Analysis of the Ego,* in 1921, Freud points out that "the ideal of ego covers the sum of all limitations that the ego must consent and, for that reason, the revocation of the ideal would necessarily be a magnificent festival to the ego, which once again could, then, feel satisfied with itself"[122]. The master, at this point, is resuming the concept of 'consciousness',

---

Theory of Libido and Narcissism. *ESB*, vol. XVI, 1996, p. 429.

119 Idem, ibidem.

120 FREUD, Sigmund (1917 [1915]). Mourning and Melancholy. *ESB*, vol. XIV, 1996, p.253.

121 VIOLANTE, Maria Lucia Vieira. The Heirs of the Oedipus Complex. In: *Freudian Essays Around the Psychosexuality.* São Paulo: via Leterra, 2004, p. 126.

122 FREUD, Sigmund (1921). Group Psychology and the Analysis of the Ego. *ESB*, vol. XVIII, 1996, p. 141.

and also the concept of 'critical instance within the ego, high-lighting its main functions, such as self-observation, the moral consciousness and the censorship.

Freud reiterates these changes in the ego when publishing *The Ego and the Id* (1923). For him, "the existence of a gradient in the ego, a differentiation within it, [...] can be called 'ideal of ego' or 'superego' [...]"[123]. Here Freud is using a concept of ideal of ego and superego as synonyms. Despite using these concepts interchangeably, he discusses the origin of the ideal of ego, emphasizing:

> The effects of the first identifications made in the most primitive childhood will be general and lasting. This leads us back to the origin of the ideal of ego; behind it lies hidden the first and most important identification of an individual, his identification with the father and his own personal prehistory[124].

In a footnote added to the paragraph quoted above, he warns that 'perhaps it would be safer to say with the parents, because before a child has achieved the definitive awareness of the difference between genders, [...] he makes no value distinction between the father and mother"[125]. In this quote, Freud is referring to the identification in the psychic constitution of the male and the male Oedipus complex.

Freud considers that "superego, however, is not simply a remnant of primitive object choices of id; it also represents an energetic formation against these choices [...]"[126]. Shortly after, Freud conceived to the 'ideal of ego' a propitiator and interdict-

---

123 FREUD, Sigmund (1923). The Ego and the Id. *ESB*, vol. XIX, 1996, p.41.
124 Idem, p. 43-44.
125 Idem, p.44.
126 Idem, p.47.

ing character, noting that "[...] this double aspect of the ideal of ego derives from the fact that the ideal of ego has the mission of repressing the Oedipus complex"[127]. This means that, in its relationship with the ego, the ideal of ego imposes rules and prohibitions to the ego. The relationship with the ego is not ended with the rule of being like the father, but also encompasses the prohibition of not being like his father is. So, the boy cannot do everything that his father does, because certain roles solely belong to the father figure.

Although Freud, in *The Ego and the Id,* uses as synonym the ideal of ego and superego concepts, Violante understands that "Freud insinuates a differentiation, when saying: 'the self-judgment [which] declares that the ego does not reach its ideal.'"[128].

In another interpretation about the emergence of the superego concept and its intrinsic relationship with the ideal of ego, Laplanche and Pontalis understand that:

> If we take the concept of superego in a broad and little differentiated sense, such as in The Ego and the Id – where, let us not forget, the term appears for the first time, it encompasses the functions of interdiction and ideal. If we keep, at least as a particular substructure, the ideal of ego, then the superego will mainly appear as an instance that embodies a law and prohibits its transgression [...][129].

In the interpretation of Roudinesco and Plon on the emergence of the superego concept on Freudian work, they also consider that:

---

127 Idem, ibidem.
128 VIOLANTE, Maria Lucia Vieira. The Heirs of the Oedipus Complex. In: *Freudian Essays Around the Psychosexuality*. São Paulo: via Leterra, 2004, p. 128.
129 LAPLANCHE, J. & PONTALIS, J-B (1967). *Vocabulary of Psychoanalysis* . São Paulo: Martins Fontes, 2001, p. 498.

It would be impossible to better situate the super-self concept, which appeared in 1923, in The Self and It. It was the result of a long development, started in 1914 in the article 'On Narcissism: An Introduction'. Freud built then the notion of ideal, substitute of the infantile narcissism and which would be, supposedly, the measuring instrument used by the self to observe himself [...] In The Self and It, the super-self is still poorly differentiated from the ideal of self, but it is considered unconscious, such as most of the self[130].

If, on one hand, the superego concept appears for the first time in the text *The Ego and the Id* (1923), on the other, when addressing the importance of the father in the superego constitution, Freud also points out that this instance "retains the father character, while, when more powerful the Oedipus complex and more quickly it succumbs to repression (under the influence of the religious education authority, school education and reading), more severe the domination of superego on ego will be later"[131]. Remember that the father, in the case of the boy, was perceived as an obstacle to the realization of his desires, and his ego was strengthened to repress these desires (as all infantile sexuality) due to the strength of the paternal law. Both in the superego and in the ideal of ego we see the moral values that have been internalized since the early childhood, since this instance can be considered a representative of the relations with the parents (here understood as father and mother) since the first moments of life. The superego, in addition to constituting the expression of the most powerful repressed drives and desires, it is also the substitute of an anxiety for the father, and this is the seed from which

130 ROUDINESCO, Elisabeth& Plon, Michel. *Dictionary of Psychoanalysis*. Rio de Janeiro: Jorge Zahar Ed., 1998, p. 744.
131 FREUD, Sigmund (1923). The Ego and the Id. *ESB*, vol. XIX, 1996, p.49.

all religions are developed. Both the religion and the morality and social sense are legacies of paternal complex.

About this heir of the Oedipus complex, Laplanche and Pontalis understand that "although the resignation to the loving and hostile oedipean desires is in the principle of superego formation, this, according to Freud, is enriched by further contributions of social and cultural requirements (education, religion morality)"[132].

When writing "*The Dissolution of the Oedipus Complex*" (1924), Freud points out that, in the resolution of the Oedipus complex, "the father or parents' authority is introjects and then forms the superego nucleus, which assumes the father severity [...]"[133]. Remember that the superego arises from an identification with the father taken as a model. And, when publishing *The Economic Problem of Masochism*, Freud adds that, in superego, "it is easily conceivable that, thanks to the de-fusion of instinct that occurs along with this introduction on the ego, the severity was increased [...]. The categorical Imperative of Kant is, so, the direct heir of the Oedipus complex"[134]. The severity that the master referred to is the superego, since this retained the strength, the severity and the inclination to supervise and punish, and such characteristics are introjected by the children ego resulting from the people responsible for their care (such as the father, mother or their substitutes), and this superego becomes cruel and hard compared to the ego.

The ego must cover "within it, as its core, a special agent: the superego. Sometimes, it is merged with superego so that we cannot distinguish between them, while, in other circumstances,

---

132 LAPLANCHE, J. & PONTALIS, J-B (1967). Vocabulary of Psychoanalysis . São Paulo: Martins Fontes, 2001, p. 498-499.

133 FREUD, Sigmund (1924). Op. cit. *ESB*, vol. XIX, 1996, p.196.

134 FREUD, Sigmund (1924). The Economic Problem of Masochism. *ESB*, vol. XIX, 1996, p. 185.

it is clearly differentiated from that"[135]. The superego, this heir of the paternal agent, maintains the ego in strict dependence, treating it as the father treated this son in his early childhood, although his severity may become a little more affable due to the mood, comforting the ego and protecting it from suffering.

In *Civilization and its Discontents,* of 1929, Freud resumes the severity present in superego, linking it with aggression. When inquiring the means used by civilization to inhibit its aggressiveness (due to the presence of hostile desire in human being), the master considers that this aggressiveness

> [...] is introjected, internalized; it is, in fact, sent back to where it came from, that is, directed towards its own ego. There, it is assumed by a part of the ego, which is placed against the rest of the ego, as superego, and then, in the form of consciousness, it is ready to put in action against the ego the same harsh aggressiveness that the ego would have liked to satisfy on other individuals, strangers to it [136].

In the excerpt quoted above, I understand that Freud is reporting to the origin of superego, linking it with the aggressiveness that is internalized by this instance and that turns back against the ego itself through an unconscious feeling of guilt. He refers to superego as an agent who can dominate the dangerous desire of the subject aggression, emphasizing that "a great change takes place only when the authority is internalized through the establishment of a superego"[137].

On the intrinsic relationship between the internalized aggressiveness and the superego constitution, Freud points out

---

135 FREUD, Sigmund (1927). The Mood. *ESB*, vol. XXI, 1996, p.167.

136 FREUD, Sigmund (1930 [1929]). Civilization and its Discontents. *ESB*, vol. XXI, 1996, p. 127.

137 Idem, p. 129.

that "the essential difference, however, is that the original severity of superego does not represent – or does not represent it so
much – the severity that from it [the object] has experienced or
which is assigned to it. This represents, before, our own aggressiveness towards it"[138]. The severity of the superego of a boy can
also be the result of the amount of punitive aggression that this
expects for his paternal figure due to the projection of his aggressive fantasies in this representative.

Regarding this severity, Freud still claims that "the experience shows us, however, that the severity of superego that a child
develops, no way, corresponds to the treatment severity which
he has already faced"[139]. The severity of this instance seems to be
independent of the environment severity where he was inserted
to, since a child raised in a way not so austere may also acquire
a very critical consciousness. His superego can acquire an inflex-
ible severity, even if this child has been raised in a mild form,
affectionate and threats and punishments have been avoided.

Freud points out that "however, it would also be wrong
to exaggerate this independence; it is not hard to be convinced
that the severity of creation also exerts a strong influence in the
formation of the child superego"[140]. Therefore, in the superego
formation, we must consider the constitutional factors and in-
fluences of the real environment, since both factors act in a com-
bined form in this critical instance constitution.

The importance of the parents in the superego formation is
resumed in the New Conferences of 1932/1933, specifically in the
31st conference named *The Dissection of Psychic Personality*. In this,
Freud postulates that "the role that is later assumed by superego is
played, at the beginning, by an external power, by the parents' authority"[141]. The superego assumes the place of the parent instance,

138 Idem, p.133.
139 Idem, ibidem.
140 Idem, ibidem.
141 FREUD, Sigmund (1933[1932]). Op. cit. *ESB*, vol. XXII, 1996,

observes, and threatens the ego in the same manner that parents did with this child. So, the superego assumes the parents' rigidity and severity, with their punitive and prohibiting function.

In this *Conference*, Freud also exposes about the psychology of the ego and its relation with superego, resuming the difference, but also revealing the close relation between the ideal of ego and superego, when he says that superego "is the vehicle of the ideal of ego, though which the ego is evaluated, which stimulates it and which demand for an always greater perfection that he strives to accomplish [...]. This ideal of ego is the precipitate of the parents' old image, the admiration expression by the perfection that the child so attributed to them"[142]. I understand that Freud imputes to the superego a function of being the ideal of ego vehicle responsible for the perfection pursuit, being the superego responsible for this ideal maintenance.

For Freud "superego is [...] the representative of all moral constraints, the lawyer of an effort inclined to perfection" [143]. In addition to the maintenance of the ideal, he assigns to superego the functions of self-observation and consciousness. While the heir to the Oedipus complex, this instance merges in the id, having intimate relations with it and relating to the outside world only through the ego.

In his reading about the concepts of the ideal of ego and superego present in this 31st Conference, Violante interprets that "the ideal of ego function is to stimulate the ego to achieve perfection and serve as an instrument through which the ego evaluates itself; and superego is the vehicle, the bearer of the ideal of ego, which functions are the self-observation, the consciousness and the maintenance of the ideal"[144].

---

p. 67.

142 Idem, p.70.

143 Idem, p.72.

144 VIOLANTE, Maria Lucia Vieira. The Heirs of the Oedipus Complex. In: *Freudian Essays Around the Psychosexuality*. São Pau-

Regarding the superego, Freud adds that "the superego of a child is, in fact, built not according to his parents' model; but of the parents' superego" [145]. The superego of a boy is, above all, a psychic instance in which the values that go beyond the parents' superego are present. In this instance the values and judgements transmitted from generation to generation are also present.

Remember that, when writing *An Outline of Psychoanalysis*, in 1938, Freud refers to superego as the "special agent in which the parental influence is extended"[146]. This parental influence includes, in its operation, in addition to the own parents' personality, the family values, the racial and national traditions transmitted by them, and also the requirements of the social environment where the individual is inserted to.

Latency Period

In the course of psychosexuality constitution, which follows the phallic phase is the latency period. If, from the psychic point of view, after the assumption of the symbolic castration, emerges an ego (non-idealized), a superego and an ideal of ego, from the point of view of sexuality, the boy enters in the latency period. During this period, Freud postulates that:

> The soul forces are erected, which, later, will appear as obstacles in the path of sexual drive and will narrow its course like dams […]. In civilized children, one has the impression that the construction of these dams is the

lo: via Leterra, 2004, p. 131.

145 FREUD, Sigmund (1933[1932]). XXXI Conference - The Dissection of the Psychic Personality. *ESB*, vol. XXII, 1996, p. 72.

146 FREUD, Sigmund (1940[1938]). Outline of Psychoanalysis. *ESB*, vol. XXIII, p.159.

work of education, and certainly the education has a lot to do with it[147].

It is in this period when the sublimations of the sexual and aggressive drives occur, that is, it is in this phase that the diversions of sexual and aggressive drives forces occur for new goals.

Regarding this moment in the psychosexual development, Freud also points out that "the sexuality normally does not progress more; on the contrary, sexual aspirations decrease forces and many things that the child did and knew are abandoned and forgotten"[148]. This period of latency ends at the end of childhood, when the adult genitality begins. So, in the latency period, libido is dormant and there is the amnesia of the first years of life due to the repression effect.

In their understanding about this period, Laplanche and Pontalis consider that this is the:

> Period that goes from infantile sexuality decline (at five or six years) until the onset of puberty, and which marks a break in the evolution of sexuality [...]. The latency period originates in the decline of the Oedipus complex; corresponds to an intensification of repression [...], to a transformation of objects investment into identifications with the parents and a development of sublimations [...]. Note that Freud speaks of a latency period, and not phase, which should be understood as follows: during the considered period, although we can observe the sexual manifestations, there is no, strictly speaking, new organization of sexuality [149].

147 FREUD, Sigmund (1905). Three Essays on the Theory of Sexuality. *ESB*, vol. VII, 1996, p.167.

148 FREUD, Sigmund (1926). The Issue of Lay Analysis. *ESB*, vol. XX, 1996, p. 204.

149 LAPLANCHE, J. & PONTALIS, J-B (1967). *Vocabulary of Psy-*

The Adult Genital Organization

After the end of the latency period, the adult genital organization is started. For Freud, "with the arrival of puberty changes that lead to infantile sexual life are introduced to his normal definitive setting"[150]. In this organization, the erogenous zones are subjected to the primacy of the genital zone. The sexual drive finds its object and is put to the service of the reproductive function.

Freud says that "only with puberty there is a clear distinction between the male and female characters"[151]. And, in a footnote added in 1915, to the *Three Essays*, Freud discusses the difference between male and female, noting that:

> "[...] it is essential to make it clear that the concepts of 'male' and 'female' [...] are among the most confusing of the science and are decomposed in at least three directions. Once the 'male' and 'female' is used in the sense of activity and passivity, once in the biological sense, and then in the sociological sense. The first of these three senses is essential, as well as the most usable in psychoanalysis"[152].

However, in the 33th Conference entitled "*Femininity*", Freud notes that it is "inappropriate to make the male behavior match with activity and the female, with passivity"[153]. In femininity, there are psychological characteristics that give preference to passive purposes, and these purposes do not match with

choanalysis . São Paulo: Martins Fontes, 2001, p. 263-264.
150 FREUD, Sigmund (1905). Three Essays on the Theory of Sexuality. *ESB*, vol. VII, 1996, p.167.
151 Idem, p. 207.
152 Idem, ibidem.
153 FREUD, Sigmund (1933[1932]). XXXIII Conference - Femininity. *ESB*, vol. XXII, 1996, p. 116.

passivity. This means that we should not equate activity with masculinity and neither passivity with femininity, distinguishing activity and passivity for active and passive purposes. In addition, for the master, we must point out the influence of the social habits which, somehow, force women to a passive situation and men to an active situation. Therefore, according to Freud, every individual shows a blend of character traits belonging to his own gender and opposite gender, showing a combination of activity and passivity.

Regarding masculinity, Bleichmar associates aspects of passivity with the ghosts of homosexuality, noting that

> [...] actuated or fantasized, homosexuality is constitutive, paradoxically, of masculinity. Defined in the game of the two sides: the originary passivity in relation to the phallic-seductive mother of the early times in life, is redefined, *a posteriori*, when the subject is structured as such and the conversion that transforms him from passive to active is produced regarding an object, which, anyway, is no longer the same to the extent that he is crossing castration. In this drive that transforms the passive into active a new difficulty is inaugurated: the male sexual identification faces the incorporation of the male genital activity attribute, paternal, dragging the libidinal remains of the originary link with the father.[154]

I understand that Bleichmar highlights a new dilemma for masculinity, since for being a man, the boy finds himself confronted with the deep contradiction of incorporating the paternal penis, granted by the father, which symbolizes his power and his masculinity, although such movement would lead him to a denial of his homosexual desire that would be reactivated by the identifi-

154 BLEICHMAR, Silvia. *In the Origins of the Psychic Subject: from Myth to History*. Porto Alegre: Artes Médicas, 1993, p.194-195.

catory introjection of this paternal attribute. So, according to this Argentinian psychoanalyst, the homosexual ghosts constituting the masculinity need to be returned to its corresponding place and analyzed, therefore, in the paradoxical movement that opens new paths for the male psychosexual constitution.

During the adult genital organization "in the psychic side it is usually towards the object to which the path had been prepared to since an early childhood [...]. The encounter of the object is, in fact a re-encounter"[155]. The object choice is performed in two moments. The first moment already occurs in early childhood and it is retained by the latency period. This choice is resumed in puberty, determining the definitive configuration of sexual life. So, the boy seeks to find in the object of the present something that allowed him to experience the sexual love of the past, but which once was banned.

Regarding the two types of object choice, the anaclitic (or link) and the narcissistic, Freud states that: "we have not concluded [...] that humans find themselves divided into two sharply differentiated groups, as their object choice conflicts with the analytic or narcissistic type [...] "[156]. This means that there is no object choice purely anaclitic or narcissistic, since both types of object choice are opened to each subject, although this may refer to one or another.

It is in puberty that "the complex [Oedipus] is relived in the unconscious and involved in new modifications"[157]. In adolescence, the young relives his Oedipus complex, reaching the adult genital organization. It is in this phase that the subject will establish, definitely, a male or female identity, because it is in puberty that there is a sharpest difference between the male and female characters.

155 FREUD, Sigmund (1905). Three Essays on the Theory of Sexuality. *ESB*, vol. VII, 1996, p. 210.

156 Idem, p. 94-95

157 FREUD, Sigmund (1924). Two Encyclopedia Articles. *ESB*, vol. XVIII, 1996, p.263.

In his understanding on the adult genital organization, Mijolla understands that "it is with the puberty sexual organization that partial drives are unified and definitely hierarchized. The child only leaves the partial drives anarchy after assuring, with puberty, the primacy of the genital area"[158].

Conclusion

The issue of the male psychic constitution in the Freudian sphere still requires a peculiar attention, since we live the age of psychiatric symptoms. Everything is reduced or closed in it. A big mistake!!! We must not forget that at the root or each symptom is the peculiar, singular, of the history of each psychic subject, and it is in this dynamic psychopathology that Freudian metapsychology falls: the role of the listening, pleasure and suffering, leads us to another clinic, a clinic where the dynamic brings us to the living drive of the patient, and it is in this drive where the libidinal and identificatory history of each one, whatever the context, create strength, life and voice. And when feeling the patient, the analyst will also enter into a world where the symptom becomes more and more secondary. Symptom, secondary formation, which this book little gave voice, but it was deliberate. We go to the subject, once again.

This subject that is constituted in the familiar-social outline, leading this double face to the symptom, and leading us to a very often questioning in Latin psychoanalytic academies: are we the fruits of the symptom, or the symptom encloses us in an alienation that we do not hear its echoes? Although the era of modern psychiatry brings new understandings about the symptomatic

---

158 MIJOLLA, Alain de. *International Dictionary of Psychoanalysis*. Translation of Álvaro Cabral. Rio de Janeiro: Imago, 2005, p.687.

understanding, in the neurotic sphere or not, no other science has ever launched new lights on the rubble of the symptoms like the Psychoanalysis. When I refer to rubble, I refer to the unique history or each one, with his desires and drives in full bloom. I could extend in a chapter on psychopathology, but performing such an act would be to condense every history that blossoms in the clinical setting inside a labeling capsule, permeating the vision of the subject from symptomatic spheres. This was not the purpose of this book, but we leave it for another time, since the clinic will always have the listening, the transference and the observation of the analyst as a guiding compass, and the basis of each patient psychic constitution is where we can find the richness of human nature. Therefore, dear reader, look to your patient and think that, from this encounter, a unique report will merge, a speech will sprout and no theory, itself, is more than a patient; since it is from this fertile ground, from this encounter of two, that the modern psychoanalytic progresses.

Bibliographical References

ABRAHAM, Karl. (1921). *Psychoanalytic Theory of Libido.* Translation of Christiano Monteiro Oiticica. 6th edition. Rio de Janeiro: Imago, 1970.

BLEICHMAR, Silvia. *In the Origins of Psychic Subject: from myth to history.* Translation of Kenia M. B. Behr. Porto Alegre: Artes Médicas, 1993.

FENICHEL, Otto (1981). *Psychoanalytic Theory of Neurosis.* Translation of Dr. Samuel Penna Reis. Rio de Janeiro: Atheneu, 1981.

FREUD, Sigmund (1892). Draft A. *Brazilian Standard Edition of the Complete Works of Sigmund Freud*, vol. III. Rio de Janeiro: Imago, 1996.

_____. (1894). Letter 18. *ESB*, vol. I. Rio de Janeiro: Imago, 1996.

_____. (1894). The Defense Neuropsychosis. *ESB*, vol. III. Rio de Janeiro: Imago, 1996.

_____. (1895[1894] a). Obsessions and Phobias: its psychic mechanism and its etiology. *ESB*, vol. I. Rio de Janeiro: Imago, 1996.

_____. (1895 [1894] b). Heredity and the Etiology of Neuroses. *ESB*, vol. III. Rio de Janeiro: Imago, 1996.

_____. (1950[1895]). Project for a Scientific Psychology. *ESB*, vol. I. Rio de Janeiro: Imago, 1996.

_____. (1896 a). New Comments on the Defense Neuropsychosis. *ESB*, vol. III. Rio de Janeiro: Imago, 1996.

_____. (1896 b). Draft K. *ESB*, vol. I. Rio de Janeiro: Imago, 1996.

_____. (1896 c). Additional Observations about the Defense Neuropsychosis. *ESB*, vol. III. Rio de Janeiro: Imago, 1996.

_____. (1896 d). Obsessions and Phobias– Its Psychic Mechanism and its Etiology. *ESB*, vol. III. Rio de Janeiro: Imago,

1996.

_____. (1897). Letter 59. *ESB*, vol. I. Rio de Janeiro: Imago, 1996.

_____. (1897). Letter 69. *ESB*, vol. I. Rio de Janeiro: Imago, 1996.

_____. (1897). Letter 71. *ESB*, vol. I. Rio de Janeiro: Imago, 1996.

_____. (1897 a). Letter 79. *ESB*, vol. I. Rio de Janeiro: Imago, 1996.

_____. (1897 b). Letter of May 2, 1897. *ESB*, vol. I. Rio de Janeiro:
Imago, 1996.

_____. (1897 c). Letter of October 15, 1897. *ESB*, vol. I. Rio de Janeiro:
Imago, 1996.

_____. (1897 d). Letter of December 22, 1897. *ESB*, vol. I. Rio de Janeiro:
Imago, 1996.

_____. (1897 e). Draft N. *ESB,* vol. I. Rio de Janeiro: Imago, 1996.

_____. (1898). The Sexuality in the Etiology of Neurosis. *ESB*, vol. III. Rio de Janeiro: Imago, 1996.

_____. (1899). Letter of December 9. *ESB*, vol. I. Rio de Janeiro: Imago, 1996.

_____. (1900). The Interpretation of Dreams. *ESB*, vol. V. Rio de Janeiro: Imago, 1996.

_____. (1905). Three Essays On the Sexuality Theory. *ESB*, vol. VII. Rio de Janeiro: Imago, 1996.

_____. (1907 a). Obsessive Acts and Religious Practices. *ESB*, vol. IX. Rio de Janeiro: Imago, 1996.

_____. (1907 b). The Sexual Enlightenment of Children. *ESB*, vol. IX. Rio de Janeiro: Imago, 1996.

_____. (1908 a). Character and Anal Eroticism. *ESB*, vol. IX. Rio de Janeiro: Imago, 1996.

_____. (1908 b). On the Sexual Theories of Children. *ESB*, vol. IX. Rio de Janeiro: Imago, 1996.

_____. (1908 c). 'Civilized" Sexual Morals and Modern Nervous Disease. *ESB*, vol. IX. Rio de Janeiro: Imago, 1996.

_____. (1909 a). Notes on a Case of Obsessional Neurosis. *ESB*, vol. X. Rio de Janeiro: Imago, 1996.

_____. (1909 b). Analysis of a Phobia in a Five-Years-Old Boy. *ESB*, vol. X. Rio de Janeiro: Imago, 1996.

_____. (1910 a). The Future Perspectives of Psychoanalytic Therapy. *ESB*, vol. VI. Rio de Janeiro: Imago, 1996.

_____. (1910 b). Sylvan Psychoanalysis. *ESB*, vol. XI. Rio de Janeiro: Imago, 1996.

_____. (1910 c). Leonardo da Vinci and a Memory of his Childhood. *ESB*, vol. XXIII. Rio de Janeiro: Imago, 1996.

_____.(1911). Formulations On the Two Principles of Mental Functioning. *ESB*, vol. XII. Rio de Janeiro: Imago, 1996.

_____. (1912). Contributions to a Debate on Masturbation. *ESB*, vol. XII. Rio de Janeiro: Imago, 1996.

_____. (1913 a). The Inclination to Obsessional Neurosis – A Contribution to the Problem of Neurosis. *ESB*, vol. XII. Rio de Janeiro: Imago, 1996.

_____. (1913 b). Totem and Taboo. *ESB*, vol. XIII. Rio de Janeiro: Imago, 1996.

_____. (1913 c). About the Beginning of the Treatment (New Recommendations On the Psychoanalysis Technique). *ESB*, vol. XII. Rio de Janeiro: Imago, 1996.

_____. (1914 a). The History of the Psychoanalytic Movement. *ESB*, vol. XIV. Rio de Janeiro: Imago, 1996.

_____. (1914 b). On Narcissism: An Introduction. *ESB*, vol. XIV. Rio de Janeiro: Imago, 1996.

_____. (1914 c). Remembering, Repeating and Elaborating. *ESB*, vol. XII. Rio de Janeiro: Imago, 1996.

_____. (1915 a). The Instincts and its Vicissitudes. *ESB*, vol. XIV. Rio de Janeiro: Imago, 1996.

_____. (1915 b). Repression. *ESB*, vol. XIV. Rio de Janeiro: Imago, 1996.

_____. (1915 c). The Unconscious. *ESB*, vol. XIV. Rio de Janeiro: Imago, 1996.

_____. (1915 d). Reflections for the times of war and death. *ESB*, vol. XIV. Rio de Janeiro: Imago, 1996.

_____. (1915 e). *Transfer Neuroses: a synthesis.* Rio de Janeiro: Imago, 1987.

_____. (1917[1916-17] a). XVI Conference – Psychoanalysis and Psychiatry. *ESB*, vol. XVI. Rio de Janeiro: Imago, 1996.

_____. (1917[1916-17] b). Conference XVII – The Sense of Symptom. *ESB*, vol. XVI. Rio de Janeiro: Imago, 1996.

_____. (1917 [1916-1917] c). XVIII Conference: Fixation in Traumas – The Unconscious. *ESB*, vol. XVI. Rio de Janeiro: Imago, 1996.

_____. (1917[1916-17] d). Conference XIX – Resistance and Repression. *ESB*, vol. XVI. Rio de Janeiro: Imago, 1996.

_____. (1917[1916-17] e). XXI Conference – The Development of Libido and Sexual Organizations. *ESB*, vol. XVI. Rio de Janeiro: Imago, 1996.

_____. (1917 [1916-1917] f). XXII Conference: Some Ideas About the Development and Regression – Etiology. *ESB*, vol. XVI. Rio de Janeiro: Imago, 1996.

_____. (1917 [1916-1917] g). XXVI Conference – The Theory of Libido and Narcissism. *ESB*, vol. XVI. Rio de Janeiro: Imago, 1996.

_____. (1917 [1915]). Mourning and Melancholy. *ESB*, vol. XIV. Rio de Janeiro: Imago, 1996.

_____. (1917). The Instinct Transformations Exemplified in Anal Eroticism. *ESB*, vol. XVII. Rio de Janeiro: Imago, 1996.

_____. (1918[1914]). History of an Infantile Neurosis. *ESB*, vol. XVII. Rio de Janeiro: Imago, 1996.

_____. (1919). 'A Child is Beaten'. A Contribution to the

Study of the Origin of Sexual Perversions. *ESB*, vol. XVII. Rio de Janeiro: Imago, 1996.

_____. (1919 [1918]). Progress Lines in Psychoanalytic Therapy. *ESB*, vol. XVII. Rio de Janeiro: Imago, 1996.

_____. (1920). Beyond the Pleasure Principle. *ESB*, vol. XVIII. Rio de Janeiro: Imago, 1996.

_____. (1921). Group Psychology and the Ego Analysis. *ESB*, vol. XVIII. Rio de Janeiro: Imago, 1996.

_____. (1923 [1922]). Two Encyclopedia Articles. *ESB*, vol. XVIII. Rio de Janeiro: Imago, 1996.

_____. (1923[1922]). A Demonic Neurosis of the 17th Century. *ESB*, vol. XIX, Rio de Janeiro: Imago, 1996.

_____. (1923 a). The Ego and the Id. *ESB*, vol. XIX. Rio de Janeiro: Imago, 1996.

_____. (1923 b). The Infantile Genital Organization: An Interpolation of Sexuality Theory. *ESB*, vol. XIX. Rio de Janeiro: Imago, 1996.

_____. (1924 a). The Masochism Economic Problem. *ESB*, vol. XIX. Rio de Janeiro: Imago, 1996.

_____. (1924 b). The Dissolution of the Oedipus Complex. *ESB*, vol. XIX. Rio de Janeiro: Imago, 1996.

_____. (1924 c). Neurosis and Psychosis. *ESB*, vol. XIX. Rio de Janeiro: Imago, 1996.

_____. (1924 d). Two Encyclopedia Articles. *ESB,* vol. XVIII. Rio de Janeiro: Imago, 1996.

_____. (1924 e). An Autobiographical Study. *ESB*, vol. XX. Rio de Janeiro: Imago, 1996.

_____. (1925). Some Psychic Consequences of Anatomical Distinction Between the Sexes. *ESB*, vol. XIX. Rio de Janeiro: Imago, 1996.

_____. (1926[1925]). Inhibitions, Symptoms and Anxiety. *ESB*, vol. XX. Rio de Janeiro: Imago, 1996.

_____. (1926). The Issue of Lay Analysis. *ESB*, vol. XX. Rio de Janeiro: Imago, 1996.

_____. (1927). The Mood. *ESB*, vol. XXI. Rio de Janeiro: Imago, 1996.

_____. (1928 [1927]). Dostoevsky and Parricide. *ESB*, vol. XXI. Rio de Janeiro: Imago, 1996.

_____. (1930[1929]). The Malaise in Civilization. *ESB*, vol. XXI. Rio de Janeiro: Imago, 1996.

_____. (1933[1932] a). Conference XXXII – Anxiety and Instinctive Life. *ESB*, vol. XXII. Rio de Janeiro: Imago, 1996.

_____. (1933[1932] b). Conference XXXI – The Dissection of Psychic Personality. *ESB*, vol. XXII. Rio de Janeiro: Imago, 1996.

_____. (1933[1932] c). XXXIII Conference - Femininity. *ESB*, vol. XXII. Rio de Janeiro: Imago, 1996.

_____. (1933[1932] d). XXXV Conference – The Issue of a *Weltanschaung. ESB*, vol. XXII. Rio de Janeiro: Imago, 1996.

_____. (1937). Constructions in Analysis. *ESB*, vol. XXIII. Rio de Janeiro: Imago, 1996.

_____ (1937). Terminable and Interminable Analysis. *ESB*, vol. XXIII. Rio de Janeiro: Imago, 1996.

_____. (1939[1934-38]). Moses and the Monotheism. *ESB*, vol. XXIII. Rio de Janeiro: Imago, 1996.

_____. (1940[1938]). Psychoanalysis Outline. *ESB*, vol. XXIII. Rio de Janeiro: Imago, 1996.

GAY, Peter (1988). *Freud: a life for our time.* Translation of Denise Bottmann. São Paulo: Companhia das Letras, 1989.

JONES, Ernst. (1989). *The Life and Work of Sigmund Freud. Vol. 1: The Formation Years and the Great Discoveries (1856-1900).* Translation of Júlio Castañon Guimarães. Rio de Janeiro: Imago, 1989.

_____. (1989). *The life and Work of Sigmund Freud. Vol. 2: The Maturity (1901-1939).* Translation of Júlio Castañon Guimarães. Rio de Janeiro: Imago, 1989.

KAUFMANN, Piere. *Encyclopedic Dictionary of Psychoanalysis:*

the legacy of Freud to Lacan. Rio de Janeiro, Jorge Zahar, 1998.

LAPLANCHE, J. & PONTALIS, J-B. (1967). *Vocabulary of Psychoanalysis* . São Paulo: Martins Fontes, 2001.

MASSON, Jeffrey. M. (1986). *The Complete Correspondence of Sigmund Freud to W. Fliess.* Translation of Vera Ribeiro. Rio de Janeiro: Imago, 1986.

MCGUIRE, William. Complete Correspondence of Sigmund Freud and Carl G. Jung. Rio de Janeiro, Imago, 1993.

MEZAN, Renato (1985). *Freud, Thinker of Culture.* 7th edition. São Paulo: Companhia das Letras, 2006.

_____. *Freud: the plot of the concepts.* 5th edition. São Paulo: Perspectiva, 2011.

_____ (1988). *The Revenge of the Sphinx: Essays on Psychoanalysis.* São Paulo: Brasiliense S. A., 1998.

MIJOLLA, Alain de. *International Dictionary of Psychoanalysis.* Translation of Álvaro Cabral. Rio de Janeiro: Imago, 2005.

ROUDINESCO, Elisabeth & PLON, Michel (1998). *Dictionary of Psychoanalysis* . Rio de Janeiro: Jorge Zahar editor, 1998.

VINÃR, Marcelo N. (2002). Psychoanalysis Today: Problems of Clinical Theory Articulation. Montevideo: Trilce, 2002.

VIOLANTE, Maria Lucia Vieira. *The Inseparability between the psychic and social dimensions in the psychic constitution of the subject.* Psicologia Revista. São Paulo, volume 19, No. 1, 2010.

_____. (2004). Freudian Essays Around the Psychosexuality. São Paulo: Via Leterra, 2004.

All data presented in this book are linked, directly or indirectly, with the doctoral thesis entitled A Theoretical Clinical Study on the Identificatory Problem in a Case of Obsessional Neurosis, which was prepared from the financing of CAPES scholarship – Brazil.